The
MAGIC BULLET

A Daily Program to Improve Every Area of Your Life

SECOND EDITION

- *more energy*
- *more money*
- *better relationships*
- *greater focus*
- *more happiness*
- *abundant prosperity*
- *improved communication*
- *more fun*
- *positive attitude*
- *people skills*

Allan R. Baylis

GLOBAL
professional
publishing

Global Professional Publishing Ltd
Random Acres, Slip Mill Lane
Hawkhurst, Cranbrook
Kent TN18 5AD
Email: publishing@gppbooks.com

Global Professional Publishing believes that the sources of information upon which the book is based are reliable, and has made every effort to ensure the complete accuracy of the text. However, neither Global Professional Publishing, the authors nor any contributors can accept any legal responsibility whatsoever for consequences that may arise from errors or omissions or any opinion or advice given.

ISBN 978-1-906403-80-5

Printed in the United Kingdom by Integrated Book Technology

This publication is designed to provide accurate and authoritative information in regard to the subject matter covered. It is sold with the understanding that neither the author nor the publisher is engaged in rendering legal, accounting, or other professional service. If legal advice or other expert assistance is required, the services of a competent professional person should be sought.
All numerical values in this book are examples subject to change. The current values may vary and may not be valid in the present economic environment.

For full details of Global Professional Publishing titles in Management, Finance and Banking see our website at:
www.gppbooks.com

Dedication

This book is dedicated to my children Laura, Gary and Cody. I thank them for changing my life and thank my wife Heather for keeping it all together

The
MAGIC BULLET

Please go to:

www.allanbaylis.com

and enter promotional number

6219

- Am I putting thought into action?
- Am I setting S.M.A.R.T. goals?
- Am I visualizing my goals?
- Am I stretching my comfort zone?
- Am I happy with what I've got?
- Am I engaging in positive self-talk?
- Am I a positive force for others?
- Are my actions consistent with my values?
- Am I staying in balance?
- Am I focused & persistent?

Contents

ACKNOWLEDGMENTS

To thank everyone would be impossible. So I'll do the impossible and say thanks to everyone. Thanks to every person who took the time to attend one of my presentations. I've always been humbled by the fact that others would take time from their busy lives to come and listen to me. Yes, I've always appreciated it and I always will.

Thanks to those who encouraged me in the early days. New friends know where you are but old friends know where you've been. After all these years I still remember every audience, the energy, the feeling that you get when it all feels right. It's my Magic Bullet. Thanks for all the encouragement and enthusiasm that I've received from too many to mention. Enthusiasm defies mathematics for when it's divided it multiplies.

Thanks to all the convention organizers, human resource people and business leaders who have given me the opportunity. Thanks also to the hotel people and shuttle drivers that I got to know so well. Many who have spent a lifetime on the road know what I mean. A life of travel brings both problems and opportunities. The greatest of opportunities are found in all the people and circumstances you meet along the way.

The greatest challenge of travel and chasing your dreams is the family you don't always have at your side. The biggest change in my life came when my kids were born. After all these years, and three grown children later it still is the most amazing thing of all. Every adult needs a child to teach for it's the way adults learn. Thanks Laura, Gary and Cody for teaching me so much.

Thanks to my wife Heather for keeping it all together. The late nights, the dinners I missed and all those extended trips. Thanks for being there at teachers meetings, baseball, soccer and basketball games often explaining why I wasn't there. Thanks for learning how to do it all without me but for never leaving me out. You've always encouraged me and have been my greatest sounding board of all. Thanks for being my best friend.

PREFACE

BRAD YOUNG,
VP OPERATIONS (*retired*)

Speedy Glass, SEATTLE WASHINGTON

I first met Allan in the summer of 1988, in Seattle Washington. I had transferred into a new region and before long I became the VP of the USA Operations, for this international retail organization. Unlike other areas of the company my region was relatively new, surrounded by fierce competition. We were the proverbial 'small fish' in the 'big pond'.

Allan had been working in other regions of our company and I had looked forward to gleaning any ideas that would help us grow in our new market. When we first met, I discovered Allan's strong belief in people. I've lost track of how many times I've heard Allan say, "companies don't make people, it is people that makes companies". Rest assured that over 20 years and hundreds of presentations later, he doesn't just say it but he means it.

Together we worked hard with the odds stacked against us, to build the best, most productive region in our organization. Allan's commitment to developing our most important and valuable asset, our people, was unwavering. He taught service providers, salespeople, managers and those in leadership roles the importance of a positive attitude and how it affected everything they did. Allan taught them to be better people. This impacted every area of their lives including our business. Our region went from being the least to the most productive region within 5 years and tripled in size before we knew it.

I believed it was important, from a leadership perspective to go into the field with Allan and attend the presentations. I believed in our mission to develop our people and I wanted them to know it. Over the years I have attended presentations across the US that Allan has delivered. He is a dynamic speaker and he presents solutions that you can apply immediately, also the ability to make it fun.

The Magic Bullet is a culmination of Allan's experiences. I have personally internalized the attitudes presented in his book and it has improved my life immensely. *The Magic Bullet* is easy to read and even easier to apply. The secret to internalization is daily application and the MDA (method of daily application) makes it easy to stay on track. This book will be the catalyst for many success stories to come. I know this to be true, as I've seen the results others have achieved and I have experienced the same. Reading and then applying *The Magic Bullet* will be the best decision you'll ever make.

INTRODUCTION

The objective of this book is to have a profound and positive effect on you. This will happen when you implement the attitudes and skills in *The Magic Bullet*. A positive impact on your business and personal life will be the result. The 21 day action oriented program is focused on implementation. This is only the beginning as internalization is the ultimate goal. When you reach the internalization stage you will feel the 'magic bullet.' You can start this program immediately. You can apply this program forever. As time passes everything will improve. The program is simple, so simple that you may not believe it. This could be part of your problem. In this book, you will find a solution.

I have invested 30 years working in a variety of organizations. Speaking at seminars and conventions, writing programs, presenting videos and implementing programs in the field is a learning experience. This book is the culmination of those experiences. I have found that when you are positively motivated, everything at work or at play is easier. My intent is to show you a way you can stay positively, motivated every day. You know what I mean, focused, high energy and happy. How you feel impacts every area of your life. Like throwing a stone into a pond, your positive attitude will have a rippling effect on others. Enthusiasm defies the laws of mathematics; when you divide it, it multiplies.

So we are clear, I'm not writing about superficial motivation. That stuff doesn't work. Haven't you noticed? You go to a seminar or read a book and get all pumped up. Then days later nothing has changed and the so called 'motivator' is gone. I'm writing about real motivation, the kind that lasts. In 15-30 minutes a day you will improve everything.

In my travels, I discovered many people are searching for the 'magic bullet.' That someone or something that will keep them 'motivated' in their pursuit of happiness. It took me years, countless experiences and several miles to find the 'magic bullet.' It's in the book.

Feeling better every day, being positively motivated is an important first step. It is not the only step. A waiter with a positive attitude who fouls up your order is not a good waiter. A positive manager who can't communicate effectively to people is not an effective manger. A positive parent who can't communicate to his children has only half the solution. Improving relevant skills is important as well.

I have written programs on customer service, sales, management, leadership, marketing, and business planning to name a few. In this information age there is so much to learn. Improving your selling skills will help you sell more. Improving your recognition skills will help you be a better parent. Improving your service skills will make your customers happy. Improving your coaching skills will help you manage more effectively. Improving your skills improves your confidence. Confidence has a direct effect on attitude.

Some people believe a positive attitude is the most important factor to achieving success. Others believe success is driven primarily by skills. I believe you need both. A positive attitude is the best place to start but improving relevant skills is an important part of a synergistic solution.

The important question is which skills are the most important ones to learn? I believe that there is one skill that is the most important of all. This skill will impact everything you do each and every day. It will make you a better parent, salesperson, manager, leader, coach, the list is endless. It's in the book.

The Magic Bullet is focused on priorities. Doing things in the right order is important. Too many people put their cart in front of their horse. This creates friction and resistance to change. Organizations have been doing so for years. This book is about you putting your horse in front of your cart and reducing friction. You want to develop a more positive attitude with real motivation, the kind that lasts. The dynamic combination of these attitudes and relevant skills will create a synergistic effect for you. This synergy of attitudes and skills working together, the total effect is greater than the sum of the parts is central to *The Magic Bullet*.

CHAPTER NONE

Welcome to the Magic Bullet

Before I get into the depth and breadth of this book I want to talk, just you and I for a few moments. I want you to have a crystal clear picture of what you're getting into. There are many books written and so much information to absorb; it can be confusing as to where to start. Right now you're in the right place. What makes this book different? The best way to explain what The Magic Bullet is by explaining what it is not. That's why I call it Chapter None.

I met a man who was a magician. He started from humble beginnings performing at kid's parties and a variety of events. Over time Magic Tom became well known and before you knew it, he had his own TV show. His show was extremely entertaining and did well for many years. As you know there is no magic. Planes don't disappear, elephants don't vanish and pretty young women aren't cut in half. Magic is all about slight of hand and illusion. In fact once you see the illusion behind the magic the so called magic quickly fades.

One day I asked Magic Tom which group was the easiest to trick. Considering his considerable experience with audience young and old, he seemed to be the best person to ask. Without hesitation he answered that the adult audience was the easiest to fool. It was easy to use slight of hand and distraction techniques with adults. He reasoned that the adult audience was too busy trying to figure out the magic trick. Their complicated thinking process made it much easier to distract them. Kids he said were much tougher.

Aren't you tired of being tricked? Aren't we all tired of being tricked? They've been tricking us for generations. They've tricked us in every way imaginable. Toxins are placed in our food source and we are persuaded to eat them. When there is a healthy, wholesome looking woman posing as Mother Nature on the box it must be good for you. That picture of grandma on that muffin mix sure brings back memories doesn't it? They use our paranoia to trick us. When the fear of high fat raises its head the marketers have a field day. Lower fat they proclaim. Lower than what? They hide salt and sugars in our foods to addict us. Then they create a multi billion dollar weight loss industry. Most of them fail too. In the weight loss industry everyone claims to have the magic bullet. Some actors even gain weight, promote a weight loss program as they lose weight before repeating the cycle. Then they cash a different paycheque with a weight loss organization. Don't you wish you had a private chef and nutritionist to help you out each day like they do? There is a lot of money to be made in the weight loss business. These slick marketers know how to tap in to our fears and manipulate us in every way possible.

In the world of multi media it's even easier for the tricksters to fool us. Send the same message out on a repetitive basis and, over time someone will believe it. If nothing else osmosis will work. How about those images they create. Don't you wish all those friendly bank tellers you see on TV were really that friendly? Truth is the automated machines are often friendlier. You see one hour dry cleaning advertised but when you go there it's never the right hour. Have you seen these gym rats that spend six hours day training? They tell you that you'll look like them in just 20 minutes a day. Some people actually believe it. The marketers and advertisers know we're looking for instant gratification, that magic bullet. They've conditioned us that way, creating illusions to fool us. In many cases it works. That's why they keep doing it.

I'm not here to trick you. I'm here to help you. The best way to do this is to be direct. I want you to have a crystal clear picture of what the Magic Bullet is. I want to cut through the illusions, the deceptions and all that slight of hand described earlier. Remember it's what the Magic Bullet is not about that makes it different. I want to expose the myths, the illusions that hold you back. Then we will move forward.

The first myth is the myth of motivation. Many years ago men would roll into towns in covered wagons. They'd gather a curious audience and extol the virtues of the snake oil they were selling. These slick presenters would make bold claims about their special products; sell false hope and move on to the next town.

Today they don't use covered wagons to sell snake oil. They fly around the country in first class and take limousines to the meeting. These self-described motivational gurus dance around the stage and get the audience excited. They sell books and self help programs in a variety of formats. This is their snake oil. Motivation is the snake oil of our generation. The sad truth is that many, with sincere intent believe these false prophets have the magic bullet. Some followers actually believe these motivational gurus have magical, mystical powers. They want to get close so the magic dust will somehow inspire them.

Many of these self proclaimed motivational, self-help gurus are masters of manipulation. They convince people to walk on coals, deprive themselves and go through a variety of ridiculous exercises. They do this in pursuit of their singular goal. They want to put money in their pockets. The process they employ gets out of control at times. You may have heard that recently there was a tragedy in the desert in Arizona. One of these so called self-help gurus convinced people to pay $1500.00 dollars to attend a three day workshop. As part of the workshop he had participants sit in a sweat lodge where they endured extreme heat and dehydration.

When the heat became intolerable some became faint. As the heat took its toll people began vomiting. Some wanted to leave the lodge. Their motivational guru encouraged them to stay and focus on mind over matter. He used guilt and fear to manipulate them. Many became ill and tragically some died. Their leader escaped in his air conditioned car. Later the participants were asked why they stayed and suffered such torment. They answered that they didn't want to disappoint their leader. The snake oil salesman is in jail where he belongs but he'll get out. The three lives that were wasted on his snake oil are gone forever.

I mentioned earlier you need to know what The Magic Bullet is not about. It is not about external motivation for two reasons. It doesn't work and you don't need it. Superficial is motivation is ineffective and often counter productive. Have you ever attended one of these motivational presentations? The Speaker gets the audience all wound up and you leave feeling pumped and ready to go. Then days later nothing has changed and the motivator is gone. Same effect you get from eating a candy bar. The short term sugar spike gives you sudden energy but the long term result is fatigue.

I can best describe what real motivation is by relaying an experience I had years ago. I've been a professional Speaker for 25 years and have travelled extensively. I have spoken to every type of audience you can imagine. I was about to do a two hour presentation for Kraft Foods in San Diego, California.

The three day conference was near an end and as usual I was the last Speaker of the meetings. Although it is what I do it is always a challenge when you're last. It had been a long three days; people were tired and anxious to return to their homes. The organization and all those involved wanted the audience to be energized. They want their people to feel good about their overall experience. There is a huge difference between inspiration and superficial motivation.

At 3PM and I'm standing behind the curtain looking out at a sea of 3,000 people. Along side me is the President of the organization. As I was being introduced he leaned over and asked if I was ready? It seemed like a strange question given the time and circumstance but I responded immediately. I looked at him and responded I was born ready. I proceeded to walk on stage. I thought of what I said and I stopped. I didn't want him to think I was one of those egomaniacs who believe he's better than someone else.

I explained to the audience what had happened and why I told Daryl that I was born ready. I further explained that I was not the exclusive proprietor of this gift. I believe everyone was born ready. You and I were born 100% naturally motivated. We are programmed to succeed. Allow me to explain. Years ago friends of mine had their first child. There is nothing in life as exciting as a new life. Their excitement was tempered by the fact that their newborn was premature. It was close for a while but she made it. When all had stabilized I bought them a plaque with my favourite words engraved on it. Every adult needs a child to teach it's the way adults learn.

Perhaps you've had a child and if not you probably will. Ask yourself did you have to motivate your child to walk? Your baby crawls and then tries to walk. Sometimes much to your chagrin he falls and cuts his skin. Nevertheless after the odd bruise and a few tears later he walks. You didn't have to motivate your baby. Just like you he was born 100% naturally motivated. Some time later he mutters some sounds. Every Dad remembers their first dada as if it were yesterday. You didn't have to motivate the baby to talk did you? Before you know it that child you were so anxious to hear the first words from is talking your ear off. It is amazing isn't it? We were born 100% naturally motivated to succeed.

Now think back to that new baby. What fears was your baby born with? Have you ever seen a baby with the fear of failure or success? Have you seen a baby with the fear of rejection? The reality is babies; you and I weren't born with any of these fears. It's amazing isn't it? Children are fearless. We were all born fearless. So what happened? What happened is we have had fear programmed in. The same fears used to manipulate us. There is fear of, rejection, failure, success, weight loss, weight gain, hair loss, aging, loss, gain, cholesterol and the like. The list is endless!

The marketers and snake oil salesmen learn how to tap into these fears to manipulate and exploit. There are many examples I can use but the fear of aging has always fascinated me. Those in the multi billion dollar cosmetic industry are experts at mining the fear of aging. Usually women are their prime targets. Massive advertising budgets and infomercials make bold claims about a variety of skin products. They continue positioning their products as the magic bullet in the war against aging. They leave no stone unturned.

I've been married for 34 years to my one and only wife Heather. I say one and only because some relationship gurus flogging programs have been married 5 times. They add up the years so it sounds better. It's interesting how it works in our cosmetic world. Perhaps you've had this experience. You meet someone you find attractive. As you get to know them a metamorphosis takes place. In time they start to look better to you in some cases they start to look worse. You know what I mean.

I am fortunate my wife is attractive. As you get to know her, she looks better every day. Her personality, kindness, sincerity and positive energy make her more beautiful to me than when we first met 35 years ago. After all these years and all my travels she is still the best person I've ever known.

Still the marketers, the fear mongers and snake oil salesmen get to her. Some nights she has so much lotion and cream on her body that she slides out of bed on me. I think I tore a muscle one night trying to catch her as she slid by. Yes I'll admit it there I am lined up at Christmas time paying a hundred dollars for 6 ounces of colored horse urine in a bottle worth more than the contents. That's another fear all together.

These fears have been programmed over time. These fears hold you back. They erode your enthusiasm and block your creativity. These fears are used to manipulate you. It is fear that stifles natural motivation that you were born with. Your fears are like weeds in your garden. You may plant the most beautiful flowers in the best soil and under the best conditions. You soon discover that it takes a lot of work to grow a beautiful flower. You also learn that it takes no effort to grow weeds. The question is if you leave weeds and flowers in the same garden who will win? I know that you know the answer.

I call this Chapter None for a reason. The Magic Bullet is not about external motivation that is short term and counterproductive. The Magic Bullet is about real motivation, the lasting kind that will take you to levels you've never reached before. You will win because on a daily basis you will kill your fears, remove the weeds and allow your natural motivation to take over. If you don't kill your fears they will kill you.

Superficial motivation is a myth but not the only one. The myth of positive thinking is found everywhere. There have been thousands of books, programs, seminars and workshops devoted to this subject. Believers rationalize that when you think positively the world is your oyster. A plethora of books have been written on the subject. I see another book on positive thinking I think I'm going to puke.

Please understand where I'm coming from. I'm not suggesting that positive thinking isn't a good thing. It is my sincere belief, based on experience that positive thinking is not the cause of real motivation. It is simply the effect. It is the chronology that makes the difference. If positive thinking is the effect what is the cause? Where does the process begin? What is the catalyst? The answer is emotion.

At the end of the day we are emotional beings. We have four basic emotions mad, sad, glad and scared. Other descriptions anger, fear, and paranoia, happy fall into one of the categories. Our first instincts are emotional not cerebral. We ask someone how they are doing and they respond they feel fine.

Feeling overrides thought. Have you ever felt down or depressed? A friend with the best intent tells you need to get up and get active. You are bombarded with logical ideas. Problem is you already knew that. It's the feelings that hold you back from taking action and doing what needs to be done. Here is the way it really works. When you feel good you think well.

When you think well you act well. When you act well on a re-petitive basis you form positive habits. When you form positive habits you succeed in business and in life. We'll get into more detail on this in Chapter One.

The Magic Bullet is not about positive thinking. Positive think-ing is the outcome. The Magic Bullet is about positive feeling. Through child like daily repetition you will feel better. An MDA, method of daily application will keep you on track. I don't write books for reading only. Implementation will bring results. The only person who will help you feel better each and every day is you. You are the Magic Bullet! When you feel better you will think better and repeat positive actions. These positive actions will form positive daily habits. Within 21 days you will feel the Magic Bullet as you internalize the attitudes presented. Positive thinking is the cart but positive feeling is the horse that pulls it.

The first myth is external motivation. The second myth is posi-tive thinking. The third myth is that a focus on skills maximiz-es results. Organizations have been pumping time, energy and money into customer service skill training for decades. They often force feed their people with a variety of service tactics. Do you find the service levels better or worse? Skill training is important but without a learning attitude the skills are irrel-evant. Organizations want customers who come back. Almost two thirds of customers don't come back for one reason. That one reason is they perceive an attitude of indifference. This is not a skill of indifference but an attitude of indifference. I have recognized this problem for many years and turned the prob-lem into opportunity.

I invest considerable time and effort helping companies increase market share and ultimately profitability. My goal is to help organizations improve per person production. Companies don't make people but people do make companies. I'm sure you've heard of the 80/20 rule. The average person invests 80% of his or her time focused on areas that brings 20% of the results and 20% on what brings 80% of the results. Business leaders are in general obsessed with a focus on skills. They see skill enhancement as their magic bullet for increased productivity. In most organizations the heat is on when it comes to issues related to productivity.

Years ago I had a meeting with a Sales Manager. He was in the car business. He was focused on more sales and wanted help. He thought the sales group were in need additional closing skills. He probably believed the ten closing techniques they were using to manipulate customers weren't enough.

I asked the Sales Manager to go through a simple exercise with me. I'll ask you to do the same later. I asked him to describe his two most productive salespeople. This would apply to any role a service provider, teacher, and lawyer. In this case we focused on his sales team. As he described each person he used words like friendly, energetic, and reliable. I made a long list of the words he used. I then suggested we reviewed each one. I asked him to tell me which attributes he described were skills and which were attitudes. Over 90% of his list described attitudes. I asked him if 90% of his list was attitudes then why was he so focused on skill. I pointed out the deadly game called follow the follower. I suggested he could blindly march forward focused on the wrong priorities. Sometimes you can do things right, but not do the right things.

I then asked him to walk me around the lot so I could meet and observe his sales team. As we walked there was much for the trained eye to see. I noticed many had low self esteem by simply watching their demeanour and posture. Why wouldn't their self esteem be low when people are telling them different ways to trick others? When you trick others you also trick yourself. This erodes self-esteem.

As the conversation continued he went back to closing more sales. He believed his sales team weren't aggressive enough and asking for the sale. I asked if he knew why they weren't asking for the sale. It was the why that mattered. It is always the why that matters. Know the why and you'll find the solution. I went on to explain to him why his band aid solution of acquiring more closing techniques wouldn't solve the problem. I explained that those with low self esteem won't ask for the order if you gave them another 10 ways to ask. It had nothing to do with their closing skills and everything to do with low self esteem and fear. People with low self esteem don't ask because they don't know how, they don't ask because they fear rejection. This fear of rejection magnifies over time and has dire consequences.

I explained further that if we focused on helping his sales team with self-esteem issues the fear of rejection would go away or at least diminish, and they'd ask more. We focused on self esteem issues and guess what sales increased. In the preface in my book a VP of Operations that I worked with for many years had his organization triple in size and become the most profitable in the world using the same approach.

This is a sales example but it could be any industry or profession. As I mentioned earlier I have worked in every kind of organization you can imagine. The products, services and methods of delivery may vary but there is one common denominator. The common denominator is people. I learned a long time ago that when you first develop a learning attitude it is much easier to implement relevant skills. When the chronology and focus are right a synergistic effect is created.

Some things change and some stay the same. I mentioned the 80/20 rule. The best resource any organization has is their human resource, people. The amount of time, energy and money organizations waste is incalculable. The truth is most organizations spend 90% of their time and energy focused on a variety of skills. They rarely invest the time, energy and money on personal growth initiatives. This is where they'd get a much larger return on their investment.

Over the years I have discovered in my consulting practice that the best way to help an organization is to tell it like it is and not worry about the outcome. I'll give you an example that I recall, like it was yesterday. Years ago I was flown in to meet the President of a large organization. The organization had annual sales of 14 billion dollars. The President complete with chauffer and limousine was a powerful man. He had called based on a referral. He wanted me to discuss some customer service initiatives. In addition he wanted me to attend the annual meeting and provide objective feedback.

I arrived a day before the annual meeting and was chauffeured to the President's office for a one on one meeting. Once the formalities were over he brought up some customer service issues. Our customers are king he proclaimed and there was a lot of room for improvement in the field. He voiced concerns about poor phone response and that he had received negative feedback from customers. He recognized such poor response was having a negative impact on productivity. He paused for a moment, gave me the cold stare and asked me for an opinion.

I told Daryl my wife Heather always tells people to be careful what you ask Allan because he'll tell you the truth. The truth can be painful. I wanted to cushion the blow. He laughed and said fire away and fire away I did. I told Daryl he was complaining about phone response in the field when his own phone response was just as bad. I've called your office many times I said. The phone rang more than 3 times on many occasions and I've been put on hold without being asked. Your phone response is inconsistent and below standards. How in the world I asked can you expect your profit centres to have exceptional phone response when yours is sub par.

I remember thinking this will be a short term relationship. He paused and stared at me with those steel black eyes. I thought it was best to let him speak first. With a grin and then a chuckle he did. I've heard about you he said. Can I tell you what I've heard? My heart began to race as he continued. He had heard that I was a strong willed, opinionated pain in the butt. I asked him if I'm such an opinionated pain in the butt why he had called me. He laughed and answered that's why I called. I don't need someone to tell me what I want to hear. I want someone to tell me what I need to hear. I breathed a sigh of relief.

The next day the President gave the annual address explaining the plan and priorities for the coming year. When he spoke of human resource issues and budget items I was all ears. This organization had annual sales of 14 billion dollars. The variance for the human resource budget was 1% of 14 billion or a lot of money.

There was allocation of these funds for sales, management, leadership, presentation, procurement, customer service and a variety of other relevant skills. Not a word was spoken or a program introduced to focus on the most important human resource, people. After the meeting we met. Frankly I was dreading the question but it came anyway. So what did you think of the meeting he asked.

I answered that I believed he had his priorities backwards. I reasoned that 95% of his plan was focused on all the wrong initiatives. He too was putting the cart in front of the horse so consumed by productivity he was blind to the reality. I said I get it you spend 95% of your money teaching people how to trick others. Then you want to invest less than 5% on personal growth issues to help them with self-esteem issues. They feel this way cause they feel lousy tricking others. Do you see the vicious cycle? Can you imagine the waste?

I didn't write The Magic Bullet for multi million dollar corporations. I wrote it for you. I know it sounds crazy but I did. I've been at this a long time. It took me a long time to get this old.

Some things never go away. I grew up poor in fact I grew up hungry poor. I know what it's like to throw more water in the soup. I can remember watching my mom pretend that she was full so we would eat. I remember watching in horror when she fainted and fell to the floor due to hunger.

I also remember standing outside our local bank with an empty belly looking through the glass and seeing all that money. So near yet so far I'd think. I feel exactly the same way about you. It may not be physical hunger. Perhaps you have a hunger to achieve more. It may not be achievement hunger for I have discovered that many of the wealthiest are miserable and unhappy. It's that feeling when you feel pumped, high energy and happy that really matters. That's what the Magic Bullet is about. When you have that feeling you can achieve anything. At the end of the day you are the Magic Bullet. Take a deep breath and get ready for an adventure. Not an adventure focused on superficial motivation and these myths I discussed. A daily program focused on what really matters and that my friend is you. I'm sure you've committed to many things in your life. Isn't it time to commit to you? I'll see you in Chapter One.

CHAPTER 1

The Magic Bullet!

What is *The Magic Bullet*? The best way I can answer this question is by relaying an experience. Years ago, on the East Coast I was speaking at a conference. My presentation was in the afternoon so in the morning I went for a casual stroll. As I walked past a house, I noticed an older chap working in his yard. I said, "Hello." He responded with a smile. I noticed he was pulling a large chain towards his shop and thought I'd seize the opportunity to initiate a conversation. "Why are you pulling that chain?" I asked. He looked at me with a puzzled look and asked, "Have you ever tried to push one?" Sometimes it simply makes more sense to pull than push. You want to make sure your proverbial horse is in front of your cart and not behind it. This approach will reduce friction.

Most organizations and that means people, haven't figured this one out. They still put the cart in front of the horse. Increased friction and resistance to change has been the result. Glorious plans to improve are rarely implemented. As a result, these organizations waste human potential and capital resources, often frustrated by the lack of results.

Allow me to elaborate. There are two predominant schools of thought as to why a person is successful, happy and productive in business and in life. Some believe that success is primarily skills driven. They believe that he who has better planning, communication, marketing, management, customer service, sales, technical, leadership and/or other relevant skills will be most productive.

The other belief is that success is driven primarily by positive attitudes. They believe that he who has the best attitude wins. Show me someone with a positive attitude they say and I'll show you a happy, productive person. 'Hire on attitude and train on skills,' is their motto. Attitude is everything!

I believe both schools of thought are focused on only part of and not the whole solution. To illustrate my point, I want to ask you a couple of questions. Have you ever met someone who has tremendous knowledge and experience, yet is unsuccessful? I've seen the most knowledgeable people fail. Years of experience it seems, have developed unhealthy attitudes. As a twenty year sales guy once said, "I'm not failing, I started at the bottom and I like it here." Even with his product knowledge and experience something was holding him back. Could something be holding you back?

My next question is, have you ever met someone who has a positive attitude, yet is unsuccessful? You know the type; they get up in the morning frothing with excitement. They look in the mirror as they pump themselves up. They smile enthusiastically as they walk into the office. As one hype artist said, "I may foul up customer orders, I'm unreliable, I'm never on time, but I'm positive." With all these positive forces inside, something was holding him back. Could something be holding you back?

The Magic Bullet is based on a simple belief. You need to have a positive attitude and excellent people skills to succeed. One without the other is not enough. Like apple pie and ice cream, they go together. There is a synergy created when you focus on improving attitudes and skills. When attitudes and skills work together the total effect is greater than the sum of the parts.

It is also fundamental that a learning attitude is developed first. This will maximize the internalization of important skills. Doing things in the right order is important. This will reduce friction. When a learning attitude is developed first, the implementation of skills is easier. There has been and there still is an over emphasis on skill development. There has been little emphasis if any, placed on developing the most positive, learning based attitudes. It took me years to figure this one out.

In my early years, I believed that success was driven primarily by skills. I was not alone. Operational gurus in organizations everywhere dedicated significant funds to increasing productivity. They were fuelled by the belief that he who has the most skills wins. I believed as well. As a result, I developed step-by-step programs for everything from customer service to sales, management, leadership, and a variety of others.

The first program I wrote in the early eighties was a three day workshop titled Fortunes Unlimited (FUN). This program focused on relevant skills. The premise of the FUN program was simple. Participants were presented with a smorgasbord of systems and techniques. Then they were asked to choose the techniques and systems that they believed would work for them. If they wanted it, I had a step-by-step system. The program was logical. I had researched and measured every technique. I knew that when these systems and techniques were put to the test, each person would improve their business. Some did improve in a very dramatic fashion, but my lesson was about to begin.

One year, I measured the results of the FUN program in the field. I was shocked and disappointed with what I discovered. I found that approximately 10% of the attendees had made dramatic improvements and had achieved significant results. When we met I was filled with mixed emotions. You know that feeling; you're torn two ways at the same time. A friend of mine describes mixed emotions as watching his mother-in-law going over a cliff in his new car. My mixed emotions grew as they relayed how the program was so easy to implement. Some said it was the best investment they had ever made. I was pumped! They were happy with the program and the results. It validated the content in the program to them and me.

When I met with those who hadn't implemented the program they weren't quite as happy. It's strange how that works. I started thinking more and more each day and questions continued to race through my mind. Why would someone spend three days at a program, leave committed to taking action and ultimately fail to implement? How about all those steps and systems I presented and don't they remember that numbers game?

Since I've never met a person who wanted to fail, I had many questions. Why do some people implement and some do not? How can two people hear the same message and react so differently? I did some additional research and was even more dismayed with what I found. My competitors spoke of the 5% rule. There was a general consensus that 5% at best will implement. Only 5% I thought. This didn't make sense to me. That question children always ask continued to swirl around in my mind. You know the one? "Why?"

This question took me on a journey of discovery. My journey of discovery is this book. I discovered that most people were looking for that 'magic bullet' and so was I. Many are still looking. They share a common belief that there must be someone or something that will keep them 'motivated' every day. They go to seminars, hire coaches, read books, buy things, and pursue relationships looking for that 'magic bullet.' They know how easy it is when they feel motivated. Imagine if they could capture that feeling every day? You know that feeling positive, focused, high energy and happy. Where is that 'magic bullet' so many seek?

Here is what I discovered. It is also what I truly believe. No speaker, trainer, motivator, teacher, manager, relationship or thing can motivate you. Only you can motivate you. You are the 'magic bullet.' You need the tools to keep yourself motivated every day. There are negative forces trying to hold you back. These forces are all around and in some cases inside you. It's time for you to take control of your attitude. Imagine what you'll accomplish feeling positively, motivated every day, not relying on something or someone else.

This is your life; it is not a dress rehearsal. When your attitude is right, the implementation of skills is easier. You want to develop a learning based attitude and implement the ideas that you believe in. You want to put your horse in front of your cart. You'll have less friction this way. There is something else to consider.

In one of my videos I tell a story about time. A friend of mine has a daughter. She was six years old at the time. She was one of those children who always got up earlier than her parents. She loved to hear the grandfather clock in the hallway and count along with it, on the hour. One Saturday morning their young daughter sat ready and close to the clock prepared to count along with the chimes. The clock reached 8:00AM and she began to count along 1, 2, 3, 4, 5, 6, 7, 8, and then when the clock struck 9 the old grandfather clock broke. The chime continued 10, 11, 12, 13, 14 and 15 as she counted along. Suddenly, she raced into her parent's room screaming, "Mommy, Daddy, you better get up quick. It's never been later than it is right now!" Whoever you are, whatever your age, wherever you are and whatever you do, for you too, it has never been later than it is right now. The time to take action is now.

Try this exercise. Think of a person you like and respect. This could be a salesperson, a manager, a leader, a friend, or a teacher. Take a pen and a piece of paper and write down as many words as you can to describe this person. These words can be anything from punctual to friendly, it's your choice. Once you've written your list, go back and put an S beside those things you believe are skills and put an A beside those you believe are attitudes. Chances are you'll have more A's than S's on your list. Attitude isn't everything, but it's the best place to start.

Important attitudes first, then relevant skills will be presented in this book. Please do not read this book like a novel. Read each chapter carefully and take notes. A short pencil is better than a long memory.

This book is about you taking action. In the attitudinal portion of the book you will be given an MDA or method of daily application you can use instantly. Daily repetition will lead you to your ultimate goal of internalization. Fifteen minutes a day will change your life.

When you combine these attitudes with relevant people skills you will feel the synergy created. The sum of the two is greater than the sum of the parts. This synergy will create new energy; *The Magic Bullet!*

All you need to do is turn the page...

MAGIC BULLETS

- There is a synergy created when you focus on Attitudes and Skills.

- Real, long lasting motivation comes from within.

- A learning attitude makes it easier to implement skills.

- Internalization is your ultimate goal.

- It's never been later than it is right now.

CHAPTER 2

Attitude isn't everything but it's the best place to start!

The objective of *The Magic Bullet* is to help you develop a healthier, more positive attitude. Have you ever had this experience? You go to a seminar and hear an idea that makes perfect sense to you. You know the idea will work and you race out of the meeting confident and committed to taking action. Driving home you think of the possibilities and imagine the results. Your self-talk, that person inside your mind, is churning with ideas.

We go ahead in time. Two weeks have quickly passed and nothing has changed. Your credit card bill came in and someone almost ran over the neighbors' cat. They missed the cat but knocked over your garbage. The garbage can scratched your car. You had to get your car repaired. Your middle child had a bad report card. Life goes on, nothing has changed and that great idea that you knew would work for you, seems so far away to you now. There is no value. You realize value when you implement. You feel the magic when you internalize.

This book is about you taking action, one day at a time. In the following chapters you'll be presented with positive attitudes and relevant skills. Your challenge will be to internalize them. A method of daily application (MDA) will help you internalize these attitudes and stay focused. With *The Magic Bullet* you implement and succeed one day at a time. In order to internalize the attitudes presented you want to practice self motivation each day for a minimum of 21 consecutive days. Daily, child like repetition will help you internalize these attitudes. Yes, three weeks will change your life!

Your attitude is a result of all of your life experiences. Some people, based on environment and a variety of circumstances get off to a better start and experience positive adjustments. Others, less fortunate have been influenced by negative forces resulting in negative adjustments. Your life experiences with these positive and negative forces have adjusted your attitude. Today, right now that is all history. Regardless of your experiences, positive or negative where you are at is where you are now. This is where we'll start.

Have you ever attended one of these 'motivational programs' and left the room all pumped up? How did you feel days later when nothing had changed? These 'motivational programs' often have the same effect you get from eating a candy bar. There's the short term sugar energy boost and then you feel the long term effects. Later, you lose energy and the sugar rots your teeth. The motivator got you excited but the message has passed and the motivator is gone. It doesn't work and the end result is nothing has changed. External attempts at motivation won't work for you for the long term. Internal motivation will. The only person who can motivate you is you. When the speaker, teacher or motivator is gone you'll still be there.

In the attitudinal portion of the book you'll be given a method of daily application. This way you can focus on self motivation each day. Each attitude presented will be followed by a question for you to focus on three times a day. These constant daily reminders will help you adjust your attitude and stay on track. You will experience changes within 21 consecutive days and the longer you continue the greater the impact.

The ten attitudes presented are in no order of importance. Certain attitudes will be more relevant to you than others. This depends in large part on your personality and experiences. Later you will be asked to prioritize these attitudes. This will help you focus on what's important to you. The daily application of these attitudes will make a huge difference in your business and personal life. Once again this is not a novel. The goal here is action. Implementation is your greatest challenge. You need to commit a minimum of 21 consecutive days and apply 'child like repetition' to internalize these attitudes. Attitude isn't everything, but it is a great place to start.

We live in an increasingly complex world but I believe it's the simple things that work. It is the implementation of simple ideas that makes the difference between success and mediocrity. Here is an example to illustrate my point.

I've had the opportunity to create and implement sales, management and service systems for a number of organizations. To make a long story short I've worked in most industries. Although these industries represent a variety of services and products, they all have one thing in common. The common denominator is people. In one of my contracts I had been working in the US region of an international organization since 1989. Over the years we had tripled in size. Gradually this region became the leader in sales, per store in North America.

In another region of the organization many miles away, things hadn't gone so well. The region was down in sales and losing three million dollars per year. The President of the company was freaking out and wanted to meet with me. We met to discuss the issues in 1998. In our conversation the President asked me to focus my attention on this region and as he put it, 'stabilize' the situation. I'm thinking, when you're losing three million dollars a year, stabilization is not the answer! He says 5% growth in sales the first year will make him happy. I'm thinking, he'll be thrilled when he sees 15%. I say few words with my plan ready to go. For you complex thinkers I warn you this will disappoint you. There is a method to my madness. Success is easy; it's the implementation that is hard.

I invested 110 days a year for three consecutive years, implementing a program designed to increase sales, improve service and reduce losses. Over three years this region recovered thanks to improved service and increased sales. The improvement in sales was so significant that the President and the usual entourage flew thousands of miles to be there for the famous victory celebration. These meetings are better known as an opportunity for the people in head office to take credit for what the people in the field do. You may know how that works. Nevertheless, it was a high powered, fun meeting. Sales had increased by 30% and momentum was building.

The marketing gurus from head office were there dying to 'pick my brain.' They pondered I'm sure about the demographics or the psychographics of the region. Perhaps they wondered if I had developed a new marketing ploy to launch a unique selling proposition. Was it well targeted advertising? What was the hook they must have thought?

With all their eager questions there wasn't much in my brain to pick. It only took 10 minutes to explain the plan. They were flabbergasted with what they heard. That couldn't work it's too simple one exclaimed! It did work because it is simple I snarled back! Better still I had the numbers to support my claims.

Keeping it simple was the key. It still is! I'm sure you've heard of the KISS principle that says keep it simple. Adults have difficulty applying the KISS principle. Magicians will tell you that children are challenging audiences as they notice the simple things and are not easily fooled. Magic tricks are much easier with adults who continually complicate things. As a result, adults are easily confused by illusion or slight of hand. Adults tend to confuse things. Don't let them confuse you. It is the implementation of simple things that will lead you to greatness.

I want to describe the plan, not for bragging rights but to make my point. Here was the scenario. A region in an international organization suffered significant losses over a five year period. There were fifty retail stores in this region. The goal was to create and implement a plan to turn the region around.

First a little background on the business. In a very competitive environment potential customers would call one of the fifty store locations compare prices, services and discounts with those of our competitors then hopefully make appointments. An appointment translated into a sale. We began measuring the volume of calls at each store to figure out the call to appointment ratio. It's the same way I work with kids in baseball. First we figure out the batting average then we work to improve it. If you can't measure it you can't manage it.

As you can imagine the batting average or call to appointment ratio in most stores was low. Once again this average was based on incoming calls and how many were converted into appointments. Let's do the math; 50 stores receive on average 30 calls per store per day or 1,500 calls daily. The stores on average convert 20% of their incoming calls into appointments resulting in 300 units of sale per day.

The initial objective was to improve the conversion rate to 30%? It was time to put thought into action. I'll spare you the details as it's the point I'm driving home here. To make a long story short we implemented programs and improved the conversion rates past our goals. This helped improved sales dramatically. This was only part of the solution.

The stores were increasing sales and averaging 450 sales regionally per day. What would happen I thought if we sent each customer a 'thank you note' after the sale? The manager would insert two business cards and the scripted 'thank you note' would assure the customer that the store would be there to help them in the future. It was time to put thought into action. Let's do the math, 450 thank you notes a day translates into approximately 125,000 thank you notes per year. I know that sending such a note is really simple. Do most companies do this? No they don't. If it's so simple then why don't they do it? Simple isn't it? The marketing gurus said this was too simple and started with their verbal diarrhea. "Do another focus group, form a committee, more research, more meetings, and more analysis," they said. They continued to meet. They are probably still meeting.

What would happen I thought when we called each customer a few days after they received their thank you note and asked them if they were happy with our products and services? How often has someone called you after the sale to make sure you were happy? Think about it, do most companies do this? No, they don't! Simple isn't it? The logic was simple. In the event a customer was unhappy we'd find out about it. If they were happy perhaps they would refer someone else. This also increased our chances of them returning in the future for additional products and services.

We'll do the math one more time. We improve the call to appointment ratio by 10% to a 30% conversion rate. We improved our batting average. We are selling 450 units per day and the stores send out 125,000 notes followed by an additional 125,000 phone contacts. So we put an additional 250,000 contacts a year into the funnel and we get more sales out. That's it, increased sales were the result. How easy can it get!

Once again I relay this experience, not for bragging rights but rather to re-enforce my point. Perhaps if I was to complicate the plan others would see me of higher value? I have written business, marketing and saturation plans. I don't want to trivialize their importance, but the reality is the solutions are simple. The solutions for this region were simple. The solutions are equally simple for you. It's not the idea that is your challenge. I know the idea works. I've seen it work with my own eyes. It is the implementation of the idea that is your greatest challenge. You are *The Magic Bullet!* Implementation which leads to internalization is the key. Are you ready for one of my favourite original quotes? "A good idea that is implemented is a thousand times better than a great idea that is not."

In the attitudinal chapters of this book you will be presented with an easy way to stay self-motivated each day. You will benefit through daily application. You will reach new heights in your business and personal life. Your challenge is that it's so simple you might not believe it. In addition, there is so much manipulative crap out there, that people are more skeptical than ever before. I want to caution you right now. The truth is this program works because it is so simple. It is the implementation of these simple things that will work for you.

Here is how the program works. In the following chapters ten attitudes will be presented. Your goal is to implement and in time internalize the positive attitudes you want. In other words, you want to make these attitudes a part of you. This will require daily application. Each of these attitudes will be explained in detail. At the end of each attitude you will find a reflective question.

In your book you will find a card with ten questions, one question for each attitude described. You want to carry this card with you everywhere for a minimum of 21 consecutive days starting now. Each and every day you want to take a few minutes and reflect on each question on your card. You'll spend more time on some questions than others. You want to practice this three times a day, once in the morning, once in the afternoon and once at night. The entire exercise will take you 15-30 minutes a day. Consistent daily repetition and reflection will help you internalize these attitudes.

That's it. You see what happens. It's so simple you think how could that work? Be careful you may be thinking like an adult. It does work because it is so simple. Here is why it will work for you. When you think of it, being 'child like' is the key to success. Child like curiosity makes you a better listener. Child like persistence helps you follow through. Child like fascination keeps you interested.

Children are born essentially fearless. You were born fearless. You are *The Magic Bullet!* How did you learn all these fears? Fear that drains your energy, fear that causes doubt, fear that stops you from taking action. There are so many fears. Many of these fears create and maintain industries.

There is the fear of aging. The cosmetic industry has preyed on this fear for years. Billions of dollars are spent on this fear annually. It has affected me! Sometimes my beautiful wife puts so many anti-aging creams on at night; I have to catch her before she slides out of bed. I think I tore my shoulder one night stopping her from sliding.

There are many fears. There's the fear of failure, the fear of success and even the fear of cholesterol. I heard of a man who was so afraid of cholesterol that he totally avoided dairy products. One day he was run over by a truck, a dairy truck to make it worse.

Fear is "false evidence that appears real." Fear is usually false but sometimes it appears real to you. Fear can hold you back. Some of these fears have been re-enforced countless times in your mind. These fears can be further re-enforced by negative self-talk and false images. One thing is certain. If you don't kill your fears they will kill you.

I recall many years ago confronting a fear. My fear of rejection became apparent to a friend at a dance party during a convention gathering. He noticed that I hadn't' asked a woman to dance. When he asked me why I didn't ask I replied, "I was afraid she would say no." He looked at me and said, "Aren't you the one who says you have to kill your fears before they kill you?" The truth can really hurt sometimes. I thought about his words on many plane rides.

A month or so later at another gathering I decided to kill my fear and ask a woman to dance. There I sat and the music was playing. I looked across the dance floor and noticed three women sitting at a table. This was my opportunity to break through my comfort zone, get up, walk over and ask. My comfort zone had other ideas. It kicked in and my heart started to pound. I could feel a queasy feeling in my stomach. My mouth went dry and my tongue felt three feet thick. I could feel my body temperature increase as my hands grew moist.

As I approached the table I singled out one of the women. I looked at her with my red face and my heart pounding. My words wouldn't come out. Finally I stammered out the question. "May I have this dance?" She looked up, gave me a sour look and said, "No. I'm very particular with whom I dance with." Although I didn't get the answer I was looking for from her, it felt great to ask and it was the woman sitting beside her who said, "I'll dance with you." We danced, it wasn't as bad as I had imagined. I had no regrets. I had stretched my comfort zone and that's what really mattered.

Children learn much in their early years. Children are born to succeed. Adults are trained to fail. Children love repetition. Adults dislike repetition. I remember reading to my children. I was always fascinated with their ability to hear the same story over and over again. I recall one night when time was tight, I tried the old 'speed reading trick' turning pages as quickly as I could. Then one of my kids caught me and pointed out that I had missed pages. They had internalized the book and wanted to hear it over and over again, exactly how it was written. Children learn more at early ages due to this child like repetition. The ability to apply child like repetition is central to your success.

Your attitude has been and is influenced by many external factors. Chances are you have experienced positive and negative adjustments. In your sub-conscious mind these adjustments remain. Does it amaze you with what clarity you can recall both traumatic and exhilarating experiences in your life? Many of these profound experiences act as important reminders and adjust your attitude. Life is full of important reminders.

A death in the family reminds you that life is fragile. An illness of a friend reminds you to take better care of yourself. A car accident on the highway reminds you to slow down. Another birthday reminds you there is less time left. Good friends split up you are reminded not to take your relationship for granted. Life is full of reminders that adjust your attitude.

The challenge is that these reminders or adjustments happen infrequently. As a result these profound reminders soon fall out of sight. Life gets in the way and you retreat back to established comfort zones and habits. The answer to growing a better attitude is to adjust your attitude every day. In this way, you will have an increased awareness of these profound reminders. This is where child like repetition plays an important role.

Life is full of routines. You get up in the morning and go through your routine. Usually the routine takes longer for women than men. Is part of your routine doing an attitudinal checkup? Imagine what will happen when you grow a better attitude? There are so many forces in this world trying to hold you back. You're not one of them, are you? You don't want to rely on outside influences adjusting your attitude. You want to take control and adjust your attitude, one day at a time.

This way you can practice self motivation, real motivation that lasts. These constant daily reminders will help you focus on positive adjustments, putting good things in and getting good things out. Remember only you can motivate you. You are *The Magic Bullet!* When you take control of your attitude it is easier to implement important skills.

MAGIC BULLETS

- Your attitude is adjusted by profound events.

- The only person who can motivate you is you.

- You need to commit for 21 consecutive days 3 times per day.

- You realize value when you implement.

- You feel *The Magic Bullet* when you internalize.

CHAPTER **3**

Use it or lose it!

Years ago, I met with many successful people who represented a variety of industries. My objective was to discover the positive attitudes that were predominant in these individuals. I later wrote and presented my second video program based on the information gathered. These ten most predominant attitudes are not presented in any particular priority in this book. You will prioritize which ones are more important to you.

Although these attitudes will not be presented in any priority, the reality is the first attitude will make or break the intent of this book. The intent is to help you implement and ultimately internalize the attitudes and skills. In this book, I'm asking you to commit to a daily plan that starts now. I'm asking you to read the enclosed card 3 times a day for a minimum of 21 consecutive days, not missing one day. In the event you miss a day, then you need to start over again.

Consistent daily child like repetition is your goal. You want to grow a more positive attitude and practice self-motivation. You want to invest 15-30 minutes each day. This will be the best investment you'll ever make. In order to benefit from this book, you want to internalize the first attitude and put thought into action. Great ideas, like flowers are everywhere. There is no shortage of great ideas. Your challenge is to implement the ones you want.

Here is an illustration to explain my point. In a meeting with 1,000 people, I'm going to introduce a simple idea. The idea presented is to send a thank you note after every initial meeting with a customer. Sending a note has little to do with skill. I use this to illustrate my point as it is something virtually anyone can do. Each person agrees the idea will work and enthusiasm runs high.

Here is the reality one month later. Of the 1,000 who agreed that the idea would work for them, approximately 5% or 50 have implemented. As a result, they are reaping the benefits. They put thought into action and achieved greater results. The only difference between the 50 who did and the 950 who did not was the group of 50 had developed the winning attitude of putting thought into action.

Again, you must ask yourself the question all children ask. They always ask, "Why?" Why wouldn't a person implement an idea that made sense? It can't be a skill issue then what is it? It's not a skill issue, it is an attitudinal one. This is where most organizations put the cart in front of the horse as they keep drilling for skills. The lack of action has nothing to do with skill and has everything to do with attitude. The first important positive attitude to internalize is the ability to put thought into action.

For many years, there has been considerable emphasis placed on the importance of positive thinking. The positive thinkers believe everything begins with thought. They believe when you think positively you act positively. This traditional thinking is missing one key factor. It doesn't begin with thought. This traditional thinking focuses on the result more than the cause. Positive thinking is the result but what is the cause of positive thinking?

The answer is feeling. How you feel determines how you think. How you think determines how you act. When you focus on your attitude on a daily basis, you will feel better. When you feel better you will think better, learning new habits and discarding old ones. When you engage in positive repetitive habits you achieve greater results. That's exactly what will happen when you take control of your attitude. As you control your attitude and implement relevant skills you will benefit from the synergy created.

The purpose of this book is to help you act on ideas that you believe in. Then you will benefit from the results. Often this is not easy. It can be challenging to go against the grain. The reality is, if you don't go against the grain you won't succeed. It's really simple. To be successful you want to do the opposite of the majority. This majority wants you to be like them. I'm not suggesting that you want to implement every idea rather the ones that you know will work for you. With a good idea, if you don't use it -you lose it! The next time you are introduced to an idea that you believe will help you, take out a piece of paper and write this question:

What are the benefits? Write down every thing you think of and make a long list of all the benefits you'll receive. It's important to keep this list and refer to it often. Most over night successes don't happen over night and sometimes you can be easily distracted. Distraction can come in many forms. Often people you know will drag you back. When you do the opposite of the majority they will discourage you because simply put misery loves company. There are other factors we'll get to later, but step one is to list the benefits to help you stay focused. Implementing new habits is always a challenge.

The next question to write down is simple. What are my chances of success? I have a question for you. Would you fight Mike Tyson for 10 rounds for $500.00? Chances are, unless you're really broke you'd say, "Why would I do that as I can't win?" It is discouraging to take on a task where you know there is no chance of winning.

With those two questions in mind, you want to start internalizing the first attitude and act on ideas that you believe in. You want to remind yourself each day of the importance of putting thought into action. This will give you increased energy. Yes, energy! Haven't you found that what tires you isn't what you're doing but rather worrying about what hasn't been done yet? Action gives you energy just as worry takes energy away.

Key Question:

Am I Putting Thought Into Action?

MAGIC BULLETS

- The ten attitudes are in no priority, the priority is what you want it to be.

- Focus on 'child like' repetition for greater success.

- Feeling precedes thought as thought precedes action.

- Action gives you energy and a lack of action takes it away.

- Put thought into action, repeat the actions and form habits.

CHAPTER 4

Change is an Inside Job!

I remember, it was decades ago I was attending our weekly meeting. This was the opportunity for the manager to vent his frustrations, complain to those who were there about the ones who weren't and generally de-motivate us for the week. Perhaps you have had a similar experience.

Occasionally, we'd get relief when an outside speaker would come and talk to us. I say occasionally because listening to some of them was like watching paint dry. Yet still, every now and then we'd find a good one. One day a speaker spoke of something you've heard many times I'm sure; the importance and the power of setting goals. You know the old 'a man without a goal is like a ship without a rudder' analogy. "Goals give you direction," the speaker said as I listened intently. Goals help you stay on track and help you measure your progress. "Written goals," he said are the difference between success and mediocrity. As a new person it certainly made sense to me.

When the speaker left there was the meeting after the meeting. Most the experienced people scoffed at the speaker's suggestions. "He's telling you that by making a list you'll succeed," they laughed. "He's saying you'll improve your focus," they giggled. Not knowing any better I laughed along with them. Misery sure loves company doesn't it?

Sad, but true, it was many years later that I experienced the power of setting goals. The reality is the vast majority of people do not set goals. This happens for a variety of reasons. Many don't know where to start or how to do it. Many more I believe don't understand how our minds work and the impact of writing specific, measurable goals.

People with positive well adjusted attitudes are focused on their goals. Written goals create the environment for change. In order to make real, long lasting change you need to do some programming or perhaps re-programming. I don't want to get too technical here but let's examine how your mind works before discussing goal setting techniques.

Your mind has three distinct parts. Your conscious mind takes in thousands of experiences every day. There are so many of these influences and images you see. How life has changed. You are bombarded by various media wherever you go. These images and experiences pass through your conscious mind are stored in your sub-conscious mind.

Your sub-conscious can not distinguish between right and wrong, good or bad. Like a computer it simply stores data. These experiences form your perception of truth or reality. These experiences may be repeated over and over again. If a child is continually told he or she is a loser, over time this becomes the truth or the self-image of the child. You may have had a bad experience giving a speech at school. Over the years, thinking of the experience and recalling the discomfort leads you to re-live it again and again in your mind. As a result, you believe you are a poor speaker and when an opportunity to speak presents itself you may head in the opposite direction. These experiences stored in your sub-conscious mind are there forever. What is in your sub-conscious, to a large degree, controls your actions.

Another part your mind is your creative sub-conscious. Its job is to seek balance or homeostasis. When what you are doing consciously matches how you see yourself in your sub-conscious mind, the creative sub-conscious works for you. It will give you energy and drive to reach you goal. On the other hand when what you do consciously does not match with your sub-conscious mind, the creative sub-conscious works against you and your focus is soon eroded. Imagine that you are projecting an image onto a screen. In order to change the projected image you must change the image you are projecting. Change is an inside job!

Many people become frustrated when they try to apply conscious willpower to make lasting change. Although they may succeed for a short period, they soon find themselves retreating back to old habits. Many have discovered that willpower alone is not enough. You need to change your internal picture to change your external results. There is good news! You can change your internal picture in your sub-conscious mind with goal setting and other attitudes. This will make the creative sub-conscious work for you as you move towards your goals.

In this book, you will be presented with techniques you can apply daily to change your internal picture and ultimately change your external results. When your goals are written, you can use additional approaches to focus on and accelerate your goals. In order to benefit from goal setting, the first step is to write goals effectively. You want to program your sub-conscious mind with a new reality as you move forward.

There are five key components in the process of setting goals and it's best to get it right the first time. Remember the acronym SMART and that each letter has an important purpose.

The S in Smart is specific. Your mind is a missile seeking device. It does not understand generalities. You want to be as clear as possible when you write your goals. Setting a sales goal and writing, 'I will improve sales in the first quarter,' is ineffective. This goal is not specific and does not program the sub-conscious effectively. Your sub-conscious needs a specific target. It is more effective to write, 'I will sell a percentage or so many sales units in the first quarter of the year.' Similarly, writing a goal that you will lose weight in the first quarter will not work for you. You need to give your mind specific targets in this case; the exact amount of pounds or inches lost is more effective. Your mind is a missile seeking device and you want to program it exactly to hit your targets. When you visualize your goals you want a clear and specific picture.

The M in SMART is measurable. When you set your goal it gives you a foundation from which you can measure your progress. Will your sales goal be measured by volume or sales units? How will you know that you are making progress?

If your goal is weight loss, will you measure progress in terms of pounds, clothes size or inches lost? You need to determine how you'll measure your goals to stay on track. If you can't measure it, you can't manage it. You want your goals to be measurable.

The A in SMART is attainable. This is where common sense is best applied. Writing a goal, 'to triple sales in the first quarter,' will in most cases set you up to fail. Writing a goal, 'to drop 30 pounds in three weeks,' is unhealthy and can make you ill. Writing a goal, 'to run a marathon next month,' when you haven't run in ten years doesn't make sense. Set goals that are attainable taking as many variables into account as possible.

The R in SMART is relevant. Your goals need to be relevant. Your sub-conscious mind is a powerful force so you want to be careful what you ask for. If your sales goal is achieved, can your company support the increased volume and maintain service standards? Do you need to lose the weight? We have young women and men all over North America losing pounds they don't need to. Some sadly die as a result. Their goal is not relevant. It's important that your goals are relevant.

Finally, the T in SMART is tracking your goals in relation to time. Will you measure your progress daily, weekly or monthly? When you pre-determine your form of time measurement it will increase you focus and help you stay on track. Once again, whatever you measure will get better and whatever you don't measure will usually get worse.

I suggest writing 3-5 goals using the SMART steps and in the order prescribed. You can set SMART goals for anything that is important to you. You can write goals for increased sales, improved service, personal growth and family goals, the list is endless. In the balance section of the book, you'll be introduced to a number of areas to set written goals. It is your choice as to what is most important to you.

What is this power of writing goals? Like most principles of success it is simple. Have you ever had this happen to you? You need to do the grocery shopping, so you write out a long list of the foods you need to buy. When you get to the store, you can't find the list you wrote. You go into the store anyway. As you walk down the aisles, you're surprised by how many items you can remember. You only wrote the list once. When you write a goal you imprint the goal. Write it down! Write it down! Write it down! There is tremendous power in the written word.

I met a nice lady at a seminar I was presenting in San Diego, California. One of the best parts of my work is the interesting people I meet along the way. This charming woman was no exception. At the lunch break we sat together and the conversation flowed from one subject to another. She lit up when she told me of a hot date she was looking forward to on the Friday of that week. Then, with great enthusiasm she spoke of the list she had made. She had written a list for what she was wearing on this date. She was taking great care to make sure all the accessories would match. You know the routine guys, the dress, the shoes, the purse, the jewelry and so on.

Isn't it strange to you that people will make lists for the food they want to buy or the clothes they are going to wear? They make travel lists, camping lists and many other lists. Often these same people won't make a list for their lives? This is your life. This is not a dress rehearsal. Think of your goals. Now write it down, write it down, and write it down! Writing down your goals will change your life as well as others around you. Remind yourself daily with the question below and on your card.

Key Question:

Am I setting S.M.A.R.T goals?

MAGIC BULLETS

- Written, specific goals help make change happen.

- Your conscious mind takes in outside experiences and events.

- Your sub-conscious mind is not selective and it stores data, good or bad.

- Your creative sub-conscious will work for you or against you depending on how you program it.

- You need to change your internal picture if you to change your external result.

CHAPTER 5

When you see it you will believe it!

Setting SMART goals is an important first step. Written specific goals give you a target to shoot for, and the ability to measure your progress. You want to take action, implement, and then internalize attitudes that dramatically increase your chances of achieving or exceeding your goals.

Most of us are fortunate and can experience all the senses. Sight, sound, smell, taste, and touch all have an impact on us. The most predominant of your senses is sight. You tend to react more to what you see than anything else. In other words you tend to do what you see more than what you hear.

It's amazing how you can fill your mind with pictures? When you want to you can change these pictures so easily. I've taught kids how to kick a ball, without having a ball to kick. When they would practice in their minds, they'd improve. For years athletes have visualized a successful result in their respective sports. A skier visualizes a ski run before heading down the hill. A golfer visualizes a 20 foot putt going in the cup. A basketball player visualizes the ball going swoosh through the basket. A baseball player visualizes the ball leaving the pitcher's hand and making contact with a smooth, level swing.

Creative visualization is a powerful attitude that will enhance your goals and dramatically increase your chances to meet or exceed them. For you skill freaks, and I know you're out there remember I was once one too, this may seem a little weird at first. You'll get over it if you just hang in there! The good news is that you can visualize anything. You can also visualize a successful outcome every time. The clearer the picture you have and the more often you see it in your mind, the more your creative sub-conscious will work for you to achieve your goals. You will believe it when you see it!

You want to practice creative visualization every day to accelerate your goals. You'll want to make some time each day to visualize your goals. This will bring your goals to life. It will also increase your ability to stay focused on your goals. Your goals are important to you. Keep your eyes on the prize.

For most people a quiet area free of distractions works best. Breathe deeply and get into a relaxed state. Put pictures in your mind related to your goals. It's important to see yourself in the picture. You can picture yourself at your desired weight goal, feeling the extra energy. You can see yourself with more confidence, giving a presentation to a client. You can see yourself enjoying the benefits from the goals you have achieved. What you picture is what you get.

It is important to picture a successful outcome. When airline pilots are trained on simulators it is always a successful outcome they focus on. Use all your senses when visualizing your goals. Sight, smell, sound, taste and touch all contribute.

See yourself implementing a new skill. See yourself repeating 10 questions 3 times a day and internalizing new attitudes that will accelerate your progress.

What you picture is what you get. Here is my question. How are you going to get fit on the outside if you can't see yourself as fit on the inside? How are you going to be more confident on the outside if you don't see yourself as more confident on the inside? How are you going to improve that golf swing on the outside if you can't see a smooth swing on the inside? You want your creative sub-conscious to work for you and not against you. The next question is designed to remind you daily of the importance of visualizing your goals.

Key Question:

Am I visualizing my goals?

MAGIC BULLETS

- Creative visualization will bring your goals to life.
- Make quiet time and visualize your goals daily.
- See yourself in the picture with each goal.
- Use all your senses, sight, sound, smell, touch, taste.
- Always picture a successful outcome.

CHAPTER **6**

A rut is a grave with the ends knocked out!

Did you read your card today? Did you take a moment and reflect on each question? Are you thinking about your goals? Have you seen yourself in the picture? It's always a challenge to change a habit isn't it? It's so easy to retreat back to what you're used to. Even if what you're used to doing doesn't work for you, at least you're used to it right? Your comfort zone is pulling at you right now.

Don't let your comfort zone hold you back. Learn how to stretch your comfort zone and make it work for you. Often people ask if I ever get butterflies before a presentation. Public speaking ranks near the top of the fears and having butterflies, or being nervous is common. I respond to the question this way. I always have butterflies but now, they fly in formation. Getting the butterflies to work for me channels my energy and increases focus on the presentation.

Individuals with positive, well adjusted attitudes work at stretching their comfort zone. Your comfort zone can be your closest ally or your most bitter enemy. Your comfort zone can increase your chances of learning new attitudes and skills. It can also prevent you from learning any. Your comfort zone can help you increase your income. It can also cause a slump to take it away. Your comfort zone can make you action oriented. It can stop you from taking any action at all. Your comfort zone can create a rut. A rut is a grave with the ends knocked out. Your comfort zone is a powerful force. The good news is that it is you who controls your comfort zone. It's time to take control.

A comfort zone is a range of activities and behaviors in which you feel comfortable. It is an internal regulating system that at times, is necessary for survival. Think, for example of the last meeting room you were in at a hotel. In that hotel there is a heating and a cooling system, with a thermometer on the wall.

When the system was designed they created a comfort zone of a few degrees. This comfort zone was created for an important reason. Without a comfort zone the heating and cooling system would kick in every one tenth of one degree below or above the set temperature. The systems would fight each other and would be inefficient. So they build in a comfort zone and say as long as the temperature remains within 4 degrees of the set temperature of 70 degrees Fahrenheit there is dead space and no system needs to operate. Gauges in the room check the temperature and based on electronic feedback adjust when necessary.

Your comfort zone has been created over many years and based on a variety of experiences. Your comfort zone is not controlled by electronic feedback but by bio-feedback. Bio feedback is a very powerful force. Over the years, I have illustrated the power of the comfort zone and bio feedback to thousands of audiences. The power of suggestion would make their hearts beat more quickly or cause their temperature to rise.

Here is what I'd do. In the middle of a three hour presentation I'd pretend I wasn't feeling well. I'd then suggest I was going to pick one person from the audience to speak on any subject for 15 minutes. As I'd walk into the audience I'd look for a certain personality type (we'll spend more time on this subject later) maintaining eye contact as I'd walk towards that one person, watching closely for a reaction. As soon as the person recognized I was going to pick him or her things would change dramatically.

First there was that look of total fright like a deer in the headlights of a car. I could see their face flush and I could almost hear the heartbeats increase as body temperature began to rise. Then their mouth would go dry as their hands grew moist. They were experiencing physiological changes triggered only by the power of suggestion. It's easy to get this reaction when you talk about public speaking. As I wrote earlier public speaking ranks among the highest fears and the comfort zone really can kick in. Just so you know I've never made someone get up and speak.

Do you remember those early days in school when you had to give your five minute presentation? Many would write out their speech and then spend countless hours memorizing the words. Then one day it was your turn to speak and bio-feedback took over. Bio-feedback would dry out your mouth making your tongue feel three feet thick and your body temperature rise. Then there's that queasy feeling in your stomach as your heart began to race. You could almost hear your comfort zone yelling at you. "That's not like you, it's not like you to speak in public, come on back here to the comfort zone where it's nice and cozy." Your comfort zone and bio-feedback can be a powerful force.

Comfort zones are also controlled by peer pressure. Peer pressure can be overwhelming and make it difficult to go against the majority. I remember the first time I saw Oprah Winfrey on television. She had burst onto the scene and was obviously a talent. You may recall that in those days talk shows focused on bashing men and people generally whining about their situation in life. Oprah began doing the same type of show.

This proven formula had captured ratings and launched many careers. I remember seeing Oprah and thinking here we go again another show bashing men and focusing on whiners. When will someone focus on winners and not whiners I thought? As a result initially I wasn't a huge fan of Oprah. I became a big fan when she expanded the comfort zone, went against the proven trend and began focusing her shows in a new and more positive direction. I believe Oprah Winfrey is amazing.

Imagine the peer pressure and resistance she encountered when she boldly decided to take her television show in a new, more positive direction. Producers and sponsors must have freaked out when she wanted to pursue this new direction in unproven territory. It's tough to go against the grain sometimes. Nevertheless she moved forward and as a result has had a positive impact on millions of people. More than her talent I admire her courage and perseverance. Yes Oprah Winfrey is amazing!

It will take courage and perseverance for you to expand your comfort zone. To venture into areas you haven't been before. As for peer pressure you better get ready for it. Everything I will explain in this book is the exact opposite of what the majority does. Do the vast majority of people work on improving their attitude every day? Does the majority write specific, measurable goals? Do most people visualize daily? The list my friend goes on and on.

So what do you want to do? Do you want to be like the masses and stay in a rut? A rut is a grave with the ends knocked out. Do you want to live in the world of misery that's always looking for company? I suspect that you don't and that's why you are here. The truth is sometimes you need to experience a little discomfort to get more comfortable. Learning a new skill, reading a different book, changing a routine, replacing a bad habit with a good one all take courage and persistence. Each day as you reflect on this question you will get better and better opening new opportunities along the way.

Key Question:

Am I stretching my comfort zone?

MAGIC BULLETS

- Your comfort zone is a powerful force that can help or hinder your progress in personal growth.

- Peer pressure is a powerful force and misery loves company.

- To succeed you want to do the opposite of the majority.

- It takes courage to go against the grain. Change your routine.

- Stretching your comfort zone is an important part of Personal Growth.

CHAPTER 7

The pursuit of happiness!

At the end of the day life is about the pursuit of happiness. Happiness for many is hard to define. When you ask others to define happiness there are countless opinions. How would you define happiness? Some believe happiness is good health. They believe if you have your health you have everything! I ask you do you know someone in perfect health who is unhappy. Some people believe money will buy happiness. There is a long history of many problems that the wealthiest have endured. I've found that generally speaking kids from poor countries are happier than those from more affluent countries. In a poor town in Mexico you watch kids without shoes play with stones and they laugh. In North America many unhappy kids threaten suicide if they don't get another video game like their friends just bought. There are those who believe happiness is power yet many in power suffer miserably. Happiness it seems is hard to define.

I can best describe my definition of happiness based on an experience I had many years ago. I was on the West Coast speaking at a convention to about 1,500 people. My presentation was 6 hours with an hour break for lunch along with the usual breaks in the morning and afternoon.

I've always enjoyed the buzz as an audience files into a room. One moment the room is empty and then almost instantly it is full. I love to meet and mingle up to the last moment before I am introduced. It can drive the organizers crazy. They are usually all wound up at these events. They get so wound up that you'd think they were doing the presentation. Just before the meeting started I noticed a middle aged man walk into the room. I could see that he was blind. I must tell you that I've seen many tough circumstances but for me losing sight was at the top of my list.

The presentation started and as I'm speaking I'm moving around the stage scanning people in the audience, making eye contact, one person at a time. Anyone who has attended one of my seminars will tell you that I love telling jokes. I have found that humor can relieve tension and drive home key points. This makes it easier for people to remember key points and more fun to attend. I believe that good, clean humor is essential to an effective presentation. Laughing and learning, like attitudes and skills work best when served together.

As I told some of these stories and jokes I could see that the blind fellow was having a great time. He laughed so hard I thought he'd surely fall out of his chair. Later I met with him briefly at the break. I was taken back by his enthusiasm and obvious sense of humor.

At our lunch break that day one of the organizers asked me if I wanted to join the group, the next day at a local water slide park. I love water slides and with a free day between travels I enthusiastically agreed to go.

The next day was a beautiful one at the Water slide Park. I saw many of those from my session the day before. This water slide had five slides of varying degrees of difficulty. There was one particular slide which was higher and more twisted than the rest. It shot up into the sky so high that in the bright sunshine it was hard to see the platform at the top. Needless to say, it looked like a long, frightful climb and an even more dangerous descent. I sat there, psyching myself up preparing myself to go down this slide.

Moments later as I stared at this monstrous slide, I noticed the blind man with that smile on his face. He was grabbing onto the rail about to climb the stairs of the ride. My heart began to race and I didn't know what to do. Should I help him or at least warn him? I didn't want to offend him. Before I knew it he began to climb, one step at a time. I watched painfully each and every step he took up the ladder. He climbed higher and higher eventually fading out of sight. When I could no longer see him I walked over to the slide. Once there I waited anxiously at the bottom hoping to see that he'd survived the ride down.

Moments that seemed like an eternity passed until finally he came crashing down, laughing aloud as he was thrown into the turbulent water. I was really impressed and wanted to tell him so. This guy was obviously a positive force. What courage I thought! I told him how much I admired his courage, to climb all those stairs and come down the toughest slide in the park.

He turned my way, smiled and said, "Son, come with me. I want to show you something." We climbed back up the ladder to the top of the slide. As we waited in line he commented how the sun felt great on his face? "What a beautiful day." he said. When we reached the slide he said, "For this ride, I want you to close your eyes all the way down." I did so and what a rush I experienced. You should try it sometime. When we reached the bottom he laughed and said, "Its more fun with your eyes closed isn't it?" He was right. Suddenly it hit me why he was so happy. He appreciated what he had and was not focused on what he didn't have.

Happiness begins when you focus on appreciating what you have. Happiness is about feeling good and worthwhile. Do you remember when earlier I wrote about feeling coming before thought? Yes it's true, when you feel good you think well. Positive feeling is the foundation for positive thoughts.

Happy people have healthy positive attitudes and a high self-esteem. This doesn't mean you're an egomaniac or that you feel you are better than someone else. Having a high self-esteem means you feel good about you. Your attitude is driven by your self-esteem engine. High self-esteem is what you want for your children so they make good choices and avoid bad ones. I remember my days in college when a book titled, The Art of Loving was banned from our library. The premise of the book was simple. You need to love yourself before you can love someone else. A high self-esteem is the foundation on which to build healthy relationships.

I wrote earlier of how some people get off to better start than others. Some are fortunate enough to experience positive adjustments. Others unfortunately have suffered erosion in their self-esteem for a variety of reasons. This has resulted in negative adjustments. I don't want to dwell on this because where you are is where you are now. What is really important is where you go from here. You are powered by your self-esteem engine and you want to feed it daily. Here are some thoughts on how to do so.

Watch what you watch. I wrote earlier of using all your senses when visualizing your goals. Of all the senses; however, the one that has the greatest impact on you is sight. You live in a visual world and what you see has a dramatic impact on what you do. You react more to what you see more than what you hear. You want to watch what you watch!

Many years ago, I was presenting a workshop at a conference in New Orleans. In this three hour seminar I was speaking on issues related to personal growth. When speaking of negative influences to avoid I couldn't resist taking my usual verbal assault at Soap Opera shows on television. You know those shows where all the business people are evil, drink martinis all day and manipulate others. These shows where everyone has affairs weekly and most get married 6 times. You know how couples fall in love in 12 minutes in time for commercial breaks and are divorcing 12 minutes later.

As I poked fun at these shows a lady in the audience did not appreciate my point of view. She started swinging her head from side to side. I can read that non-verbal communication stuff so I stopped in the middle of the presentation to ask her why she disapproved. She went on to explain that she had watched the same show for 20 years and experienced no negative side effects? Did she you wonder? Did anyone else?

I looked at her and asked a simple question. I went on offer a reward to re-enforce my point. I told her I would give her money if she could tell me of one character in this show who wasn't in trouble or wasn't heading for trouble. A silence fell over the audience. Others in the audience, who were familiar with the show started to think about it as well. This lady was speechless. She couldn't find one such character in a show she had watched for over 20 years. There are better role models to watch.

But that's not what concerns me. Adults hopefully can sift through this visual garbage and keep things in perspective. Your life experiences give you a broader perspective. What concerns me is that little girl or boy sitting beside a parent taking all of these false images in. There he sits, with that perfect pattern memory taking all this garbage in. You control what you watch and much like throwing a stone into a pond there is a rippling effect.

Speaking of your ability to control what you watch, here's what is interesting to me. If I was to take some rotten, stinking garbage and try to dump it on your head you would never allow it to happen. You would resist. You would say, "No way am I letting you dump this stinking garbage on my head!" The question I have is, if you wouldn't let someone put garbage on your head why would you let someone or something put garbage in your head?

Living on the West Coast I've learned a few things about gardening. I've discovered that it takes a lot of work to grow a rose. You need the right soil; the right amount of sunshine really helps. You need to fertilize the rose and prune it so it grows stronger. Then there are those bugs. It takes a lot of work to grow a rose.

I've made another discovery. It doesn't take any work at all to grow weeds. The soil doesn't seem to matter nor does the amount of sunlight. You don't have to water or fertilize weeds as they just grow. Bugs it seems are never a problem. It doesn't take any work to grow a weed.

The question is if you leave the weeds and roses alone in your garden who will ultimately win? You know the answer, the weeds will win. Your mind is the greatest garden of all. You want to plant positive seeds and nurture them so they will grow. There are weeds or bad attitudes trying to get into your garden, your mind every day. It's important to fill your mind with positive thoughts daily to keep the weeds away.

It is important to watch what you watch but it is also important to watch what you read. Reading is exercise for the mind. Sadly many adults after finishing school get out of the habit of reading. When you read statistics regarding illiteracy levels in North America it is startling. Many people have never been given the opportunity to learn to read. Imagine what they are missing. When you choose not to read you have no advantage over those who cannot. It is also important to consider what to read. A book that is motivational, inspirational or educational is a great place to start. When you exercise your mind filling it with positive thoughts good things tend to happen.

Another way to fuel your self-esteem engine is with exercise. Exercise gives you more energy and creates greater clarity. A walk in the park, a swim at a pool, a sport you enjoy all have a positive effect on your self-esteem engine. Remember to consult with your doctor before starting any exercise program. As little as 20 minutes of activity a day will give you that extra energy to achieve your goals.

One of the greatest challenges you face when you focus on your self-esteem is how others will react. Yes it is true that misery loves company and others want to drag you back to their comfort zone. Have you ever met that person who's glass is always half empty. You know the type, 'psychic bleeders' who love to relive failures and disappointments of the past, one more time.

The reality is, there are people in life who give you energy and there are those who take it away. Sometimes these negative forces can be friends and associates. You have a choice to make? Do you want to be like the rest or be like the best? In order to be the best, you need to surround yourself with winners, not whiners. This may result in severing relationships that drag you down so you can spend more time with enthusiastic, supportive people. Enthusiasm defies the laws of mathematics for when you divide it will multiply. Surround yourself with positive forces whenever you can.

Goal setting as discussed earlier is also an important way to boost your self-esteem engine. Goals create a better purpose and sense of direction. This will increase your focus and personal momentum. Written, specific goals provide targets in life you can hit feeling a greater sense of accomplishment. I've witnessed personally the power of goal setting and goal setting is an important part of an improved self-esteem.

All of these methods to boost your self-esteem engine will work for you when you put thought into action. Before you get to your next Key Question: I want to re-enforce the importance of daily appreciation of what you have. Since life is the pursuit of happiness and your self-esteem plays a huge role here is something to consider.

Happy, productive people with well adjusted attitudes appreciate what they have. This law of appreciation is a powerful and positive force. I have found that when you appreciate what you have you will always get more. When you don't appreciate what you have you will always get less.

Earlier, I wrote of the importance of daily reminders so you can take control and adjust your attitude on a daily basis. You succeed or fail one day at a time. I also wrote of the importance of doing a 'check up from the neck up'. If women and men can spend an hour in the morning to get their physical act together, then why not invest 10 minutes to focus on your attitude. Taking a personal inventory each day will change your life forever.

Take a sheet of paper and make a long list of all the good things in your life. It's so easy to fall in the trap of taking things for granted. Usually it's the simple, really important things that are overlooked. When I make my list and reflect on it daily I feel great and it puts things in perspective. Years ago a friend who was a great athlete lost the use of his legs in a car accident. Eventually he received a multi million dollar settlement for the permanent loss of his legs. Would you trade the use of your legs for a million dollars? How about ten million? The things that really matter are not for sale.

In my charity work I have witnessed many things. One young girl I worked with lost the use of her arms, legs and lungs at the age of eight due to a tragic car accident. I am so thankful to have three healthy, happy children. I see every day how happy my wife of 30 years is. I know she's happy because she's always smiling when she drives me to the airport. Imagine what will happen when you focus on your list each day focusing on the positives only. Imagine how pumped you'll feel before you head off to face each day when you do your 'checkup from the neck up" each day asking yourself the next Key Question: on your card as a daily reminder.

Key Question:

Am I happy with what I've got?

MAGIC BULLETS

- Happiness for many is difficult to define. Money, power, success or health do not guarantee happiness.

- Happiness begins with appreciating what you have on a daily basis.

- Watch what you watch. Visuals have powerful effects, both positive and negative.

- Watch what you read. Read something inspirational, motivational or educational.

- Make a list of all the good things in your life and then focus daily on all the good things in your life.

CHAPTER 8

The most important conversation you'll ever have!

It is you who controls your attitude. You are *The Magic Bullet*. Your sub-conscious mind plays an important and dramatic role in the process. Positive messages sent to your sub-conscious have a positive effect and negative messages have a negative effect. Conversations you have with others will impact your attitude but the most important conversation you'll ever have is the one you're always having with yourself. You want to control your thoughts. You are what you think of most of the time.

You engage in self-talk or mind chatter all the time. You're doing it right now. You know that little person inside your mind that races along so quickly. This mind chatter happens so fast that at times it's hard to catch up. You may have experienced the frustration of trying to write quickly enough to keep up with your thoughts. A normal conversation takes place at a rate of 125-150 words per minute but your self-talk takes place at a rate of 400-600 words per minute. This on going self-talk or mind chatter will have a dramatic impact, positive or negative on your attitude.

For most people unfortunately the impact of their self-talk is negative in nature, leading to negative results. Remember that your self-talk sends a message positive or negative to your subconscious mind. Your sub-conscious mind cannot distinguish right from wrong and like a computer stores data. This stored data, in large part based on repetition, spoken or thought creates your truth or self image. When you take control of your self-talk and focus on positives good things happen. People who engage in negative self-talk are rehearsing failure and sadly they usually experience failure as a result.

I love presenting seminars to groups but sometimes it can be a challenge to get there. Once I presented 26 seminars in 27 days in three countries, the US, Canada and Great Britain. Each day I would present a six hour seminar then head to the airport and fly to my next destination. As I hopped from west to east each city was approximately a two hour flight away with the exception of the long haul to Europe. When I arrived an event organizer would usually meet me at the airport.

These organizers were aware of my hectic schedule and their first words usually went something like this. "Allan your schedule is brutal you must be so tired." When you tell yourself you're tired you'll usually tire more. I learned early in the game to look at them and say, "I'm not tired; I get more and more energy every day." You know what, after a while I did get more and more energy every day. When you focus on positive self-talk you also become more aware of the negative self-talk of others.

"I'm so unlucky!" I heard a man say. "I buy a new suit with two pair of pants and I burn a hole in my jacket." He didn't know that the biggest part of luck was in believing that he was lucky. Statements or thoughts like, "I can't stay on track, nothing works for me, I'm tired, I'm sick" and a variety of others can have a negative impact on your attitude. These thoughts and statements create a negative picture in your sub-conscious and plant seeds of failure. If you want to be successful you want to rehearse success planting the seeds of success in your mind.

Another important part of positive self-talk is realizing that you have control over how things occur. You can choose to have a positive outlook or you can choose to feel victimized by the world. People with positive attitudes recognize that they can have control over their destinies and that the paths they take are their choices. When you approach things on a "want to, choose to" basis, you get more positive results than when you feel forced into doing something. When you call a client, "because you have to" you restrictively motivate yourself. It is like you are pushing yourself around. Inwardly, you will resent it, and push back. You then might creatively avoid the situation.

Yes it is you who controls your attitude and the next question on your card practiced daily will help you internalize positive self-talk.

Key Question:

Am I filling my mind with positive self-talk?

MAGIC BULLETS

- Your most important conversation you'll ever have is the one you have with yourself.

- Learn to control your self-talk to train your sub-conscious. Avoid phrases like I can't, I'm tired, I'm unlucky etc.

- Avoid negative self-talk and learn to be aware of it.

- Your sub-conscious cannot distinguish right and wrong so only plant positive seeds.

- You have control over how things occur. Choose want to over have to.

CHAPTER 9

You help me feel good!

There are positive and negative forces in your world. One person you interact with can energize you and another, if you're not careful; can take your energy away. An important characteristic of a positive attitude is being a positive force for others. People want to be around a positive force and tend to polarize towards positive people. On the other hand people want to get away from negative forces and tend to move in the opposite direction. An important attitude to internalize is being a positive force for others.

Have you ever noticed how people are so quick to criticize and so slow to recognize? Recognition is a powerful tool that can encourage and maintain a new, positive behavior. When you are a positive force for others you are quick to recognize and destructive criticism is the last thing on your mind.

Often in my management and leadership programs I'll ask the participants if they believe recognition is an important skill to change behavior and show appreciation. After the hands go up and there is general agreement I ask the same participants to show me when and how to apply recognition. Suddenly the room goes silent. It has been my experience that less than 20% of managers know how to apply this valuable people skill. My question is if these same mangers don't apply recognition in the workplace how can they do the same at home with their spouses, friends and children? We have recognition deprivation in our society. Recognition can move mountains!

Some confuse recognition with the rah-rah hype. Hype is when someone continues to back slap with the same meaningless comments repeated over and over again. This approach may work for the short term but over time is often perceived as superficial, insincere and can be counter productive. Recognition when applied properly is a powerful people skill that managers, teachers, parents, spouses and others can use to show appreciation, change a poor behavior of re-inforce a positive one

The first step in applying recognition is to make a general reference. For example saying, "Mary, you did a great job last week." is a starting point. You can recognize someone when they exceed expectations. You can recognize someone when they continually meet expectations. You can recognize someone who meets an expectation they haven't met before. When you catch your son, daughter, fellow worker, or spouse doing something right let them know about it. You want to look for opportunities to recognize others. This is what positive force people do.

The second step to make recognition meaningful is to give a specific example of what you liked. For example you say "Mary, I noticed how you handled that unhappy customer last week and I was impressed." When you tell someone specifically what you like it makes recognition more meaningful. It also increases the chances of them repeating the desired behavior again. This works well in business and in life.

The third step is to mention the person's personal qualities. For example, "Mary, your patience and listening skills were obvious, you never lost your temper and focused on your customer." When you mention personal qualities you make it real. You have noticed what they did and that is more meaningful to the person you recognize.

The fourth and final step is to focus on the resulting benefits. For example, "Thanks to your efforts Mary that angry customer left as a happy one and will come back to us in the future. I noticed and appreciate what you did." These same four steps can be used as a parenting skill and there are a variety of situations where you can apply recognition. People who are positive forces recognize others. Recognition can move mountains and is an important skill to being a positive force for others.

Your son cut the lawn without being asked. Your daughter cleaned up the kitchen. Your spouse washed your car. Your salesperson exceeded their goals. Your receptionist is always on time. It's easy to take someone for granted. Whatever you take for granted you tend to lose. You want to look for opportunities to recognize others and be a positive force.

I believe that the people you meet and the books you read will have a dramatic impact on your life. I want to tell you of a great leader who has the important skills we'll get into later. He is also a positive force for others. I met Brad Young in 1988 in Seattle, Washington where he and his lovely wife Laura still reside. Brad went on to be the VP of Operations for a large organization and we traveled around the US together. I would venture to say, that over the years we did 100 trips together presenting workshops and working in stores in the field.

I've found that when you travel with someone you really get to know them. We were together for extended periods of time and endured the challenges of travel. When Brad met with anyone he was always enthusiastic. You could feel the power of his positive attitude. Brad is not only the best leader I have ever met he is also the most positive force I have ever seen. He'd go into the field and I'd witness his magic as he encouraged others to do better and recognized them when they did. He is a living example of how positive attitudes and people skills work well together.

Have you ever had someone in a leadership position ask you to be more positive even though they were not? Brad's positive force wasn't something that he turned on and off like a tap. He spread his positive force to co-workers, family and friends. I've known Brad for many years and I'm a better person for it. I've also met his family and they too, like their father are positive forces. Everyone wants their children to have positive, healthy attitudes. The first step in reaching that goal is to be a positive force yourself. The apples don't fall far from the tree. Like throwing a stone into a pond Brad's positive force has caused a rippling effect, affecting many people in a positive way. It may rain in Seattle but Brad brings sunshine to everyone.

Another opportunity you have to be a positive force for others is to find someone to help. There is no shortage of good causes you can give your time and energy to. I've been involved in a variety of charities over the years and although my intent was to unselfishly help someone else it has helped me more.

I remember going to sick children's hospitals and seeing things that I won't describe. I also remember going home that night and staring at my healthy baby in her crib. As I stared at her I really appreciated the blessing of her good health. I was moved by the courage of these kids. They gave me courage and hope. Many of these children had better attitudes with their disabilities than did those without. It makes you wonder who really is disabled. Find someone to help and your life will be much better for it. There is no shortage of people to help and always someone less fortunate than you. When you are a positive force for others you are also a positive force for yourself. Keep this in your mind as you ask your Key Question: each day.

Key Question:

Am I being a positive force for others?

MAGIC BULLETS

- Positive force people recognize others.

- In order to get you must give. Practice the law of reciprocity.

- Recognition encourages others to perform better.

- Positive forces give you energy. Negative forces take it away.

- Find someone to help. When you help another you help yourself.

CHAPTER 10

Do your actions match your values?

Another characteristic of a positive, healthy attitude is a strong value system. When you know what you value in life you also recognize the costs of compromise. It is often tempting in business, for example to ignore your ethical values of honesty and integrity. "Just this once," you think.

But the long-term costs are high. You erode that inner core of belief that enables you to act with confidence and conviction. When you go away from your values, you also lessen your opportunity to be a positive force for others. I wrote earlier in the goal setting section that how you act on the outside must be consistent with what you see on the inside. Your external actions need to match your inner core values to grow and maintain a positive attitude.

There are people, for example who try to make themselves or their services look better by putting down another person or company. Not only is putting others down bad style but over the long haul it will erode your self-esteem eventually draining your energy and enthusiasm. It is often tempting to ignore your values but the price you pay is high.

The next time you are challenged by any conflict of your actions with your values I want you to think of two pains. One pain is the pain of discipline. It's not easy to be disciplined, especially when you live in a world where many seek instant gratification. Have you ever driven by your local gym and had to use all the discipline you had to go inside and exercise? When you left the gym, feeling great with increased energy you were glad you did. It's not easy to be disciplined. Have you ever been out with friends, having a great time and been tempted to drink alcohol before driving home? It is not always easy to say, 'no' to that drink. It takes discipline. Imagine how many people would be alive today if you and everyone else said no to that drink paying the pain of discipline and possibly avoiding a lifetime of regret.

It is often a challenge to pay the pain of discipline. It can test your inner strength to make the right choices. The right choices are not always the easy ones. The other pain is the pain of regret. The price of the pain of discipline is high. The price of the pain of regret is much higher. Imagine a balance scale with discipline on one side and regret on the other. Every ounce of discipline you lose will cost you in pounds of regret. The laws of reciprocity work for you when you choose the pain of discipline. These same laws work against you many times more with the pain of regret.

One of the people skills I have taught many is a simple one that I call the 24 hour rule. It takes tremendous discipline to apply it. The 24 hour works this way. No matter what someone says to you, and people can say some cruel things at times, don't react for at least 24 hours. Have you ever in a fit of temper said things you wish you could take back later? I've got some news for you and that is you can't take your words back. Apply the pain of discipline and think it through for 24 hours. Give yourself time to think before you react.

I'm not suggesting you can't react what I'm saying is think about it for a minimum of 24 hours before you do. It's tough to do but I promise you that you'll feel better as a result. Many people I've worked with have told me stories and how they were glad they applied the 24 hour rule in both their business and personal life. The 24 hour rule will work for you too.

Yes for the short term discipline is tough but over the long term regret is even tougher. When you apply discipline it makes you feel good and that's what developing a positive, healthy attitude all is about. It's always important to make sure your actions are consistent with your values to grow and maintain a positive attitude. The question on your card that follows will remind you of the importance of doing so each day.

Key Question:

Are my actions consistent with my values?

MAGIC BULLETS

- When you compromise your values
  the long term costs are high.

- Putting others down is bad style
  and has long term consequences.

- Practice the 24 hour rule. Don't react for 24 hours
  to anything that bothers you.

- The pain of discipline is tough but the pain
  of regret is tougher.

- The pain of discipline cost is high. The pain
  of regret cost is higher.

CHAPTER 11

Staying in Balance!

There is a good chance that you are a baby boomer. You know the largest group of people ever born after WWII. In the event you are a baby boomer it sure is strange to be one. We boomers are all time warped. We still hear the same songs on the radio we listened to forty years ago. Marketers are always trying to appeal to us with retro cars and music. All the while Baby Boomers are getting older, moving along a lifeline like a mouse being digested in a snake's belly.

As each year passes time moves more quickly. One day you look up and there's more distance behind your cart than in front of it. Parents pass away and you lose that sense of immortality you once had. As a result many of your priorities begin to change. As these priorities change you seek more balance in your life.

Boomers grew up in a low tech environment that with exponential growth has become a fast paced, high tech environment. Those of you who are younger have lived in a high tech, fast paced environment all of your lives without the point of comparison most boomers have experienced. As a result, whether you are a boomer or not, balance is a significant issue in today's world.

Staying in balance is an important part of growing and maintaining a positive attitude. Much like the wings on an airplane if you go too far out of balance you'll usually crash. Balance is a challenge for all of us. It is easy to fall into an activity trap and get out of balance.

Balance is having time for the people and things that really count in your life. It requires taking time to step back and reflect on things from time to time. You want to set new goals and visualize them as necessary. In doing this, you become more fulfilled, well rounded and better able to respond positively to situations.

The best way to achieve balance is to set goals for those areas of your life that are most important to you. Writing goals will help you prioritize. When you set SMART goals you are making an important statement of what is really important to you. In addition goal setting helps you maintain your focus. There are many areas to which you can apply goals to achieve greater balance. What is important is to write goals that are important to you

Business or financial goals are important and necessary for most people. Contrary to popular opinion most people are not motivated by money. Most people don't take their check or commissions, cash them into dollar bills, take off their clothes and roll around in the money all weekend. However, you often need money to fulfill your other goals.

I think of having money as being able to buy tickets to go on rides. You choose your ride. Your ride could be security, a vacation, education, or joining a gym. There are many rides to choose. The reality is all these things require money so setting financial goals is important for most people. When you write SMART goals you will dramatically increase your odds of achieving or exceeding them. Then you can buy more tickets and go on more rides.

Physical goals are important. Although good health doesn't guarantee happiness it certainly helps. I remember as a youngster playing every sport possible, taking long bike rides down to the river and sneaking onto a tennis court at midnight. Things tend to change and as you age. An increased awareness of the fragility of life takes over. You look back wishing you had exercised more and had eaten the right foods.

It's never too late to start but it will take SMART written goals to get you there. Willpower is not enough as it is short term and elastic in nature. You know how that works. You avoid a certain food and then one day in a moment of weakness you eat it. Then once you've eaten guilt kicks in and you inhale them to catch up. Remember the power of your sub-conscious mind. Change is an inside job. You need to do some programming to change your internal picture. Your internal picture has been with you a long time. You'll want to work daily to change it. When you accelerate your goals with skills like visualization and positive self-talk you make long term change without the negative, rebounding effect.

Family goals are important for most of us. You are born totally dependent on someone to survive. This remains your reality for many years. At one point typically, you want to break away and distance yourself from your parents. All of a sudden they seem square. One day you leave and you're out there on your own with the feeling of your new found freedom. Soon you learn that it isn't free.

For many, one of life's biggest changes is on the way and before you know it, you have a child. Some things in life are simply indescribable and having a child is one of them. As you begin to appreciate the ultimate commitment it takes to raise a child you have a new found appreciation of what your parents did and the cycle continues.

Most dream of a better life for their family and setting SMART goals is the best way to get there. It's also the best way to ensure that those important to you develop goal setting habits early in life. In order to encourage your children to set goals you want to set goals. The best leaders lead by example. Remember that when you set written SMART goals you are saying it's important to you and helps you prioritize most effectively.

Spiritual goals are important for most people. Your faith and belief system can be central to attaining balance in your life. Your beliefs, whatever they may be, are the foundation of your self-esteem. At times, for a variety of reasons you may feel disconnected and need to re-focus. Setting SMART written spiritual goals will help you achieve greater balance. Remember when you write SMART goals you are making a strong statement. That statement is that that spiritual growth is important to you.

Personal Growth goals are important for most of us. Personal growth fuels your self-esteem engine and stretches your comfort zone. Perhaps you have lost the habit of reading and want to read more. Maybe you want to learn a new language. Perhaps you want to play an instrument or write a book.

It's easy to make a long wish list. It is also a great place to start. You need to make a long list of your wishes and stretch your comfort zone. You want to imagine the possibilities. You want to visualize the results and feel the feelings. You want to go back over your wish list and be sure what you wish is what you want. Then you want to set SMART written goals and turn your wishes into reality.

The social dimension of life is important to most people. Many claim that they want to be alone yet we all tend to live close to each other. In most things you do, you interact with people. Later in the book in the skills section, you'll learn the most important skill of all. You may already know. The people you meet and those you befriend have a dramatic impact on your life. It is true that you can pick your friends so it appears wise to have the skills for that important selection. Often you are challenged when you become disconnected from people you value. Perhaps you want to expand your comfort zone and meet new people. Maybe you want to join a club. Whatever your interests setting written goals for social activity is an important step in achieving balance.

So we are clear, you do not need to set goals for any of these areas if it is not important to you. In fact, this is an important part of the process. When you write specific goals you are affirming their importance to you. The S in SMART means that your goal needs to be specific. The M in SMART means your goal needs to be measurable. How will you measure your progress? The A in SMART means attainable, realistic goals. You need to stretch your comfort zone with your goals and make sure you can handle the desired result. The R in SMART means relevant. Will your company be able to deliver the increased business? Do you need to lose that weight? The T in SMART stands for time measured. In other words how will you track your goal will it be hourly, daily or monthly? How often from a time perspective will you review your goals?

The balance you seek is in your hands. You'll be off to the right start. Setting written goals will help you prioritize what's important to you. Your written goals will increase your focus and sense of purpose. Now you can use your written goals as your foundation to incorporate other attitudes like creative visualization, and positive self-talk on a daily basis. As you repeat this question every day 3 times a day they will act as daily reminders of the importance of balance to you. Reflect on this question and others on your card daily.

Key Question:

Am I staying in balance?

MAGIC BULLETS

- Staying in balance maintains a healthy attitude and minimizes frustration.

- Balance is achieved by setting SMART goals in all areas of your life.

- Set SMART goals in areas that are important to you.

- Make a long wish list and focus on your list daily.

- Always measure your progress. Whatever you measure gets better.

For each of the following questions, mark the appropriate box. If you feel satisfied, put an X in the "YES" box. If you feel change is needed, put an X in the "NO" box. Afterward, consider those to which you have responded "NO". Write goals (affirmations) below which will help you change. Remember that goals should be written in the present tense, in positive terms and in the first person.

Health/Physical

	YES	NO
1. Do you feel healthy?		
2. Do you have a program or regular physical exercise that you follow?		
3. Do you see your doctor for regular checkups?		
4. Are you satisfied with your energy level most of the time?		
5. Is your weight at a healthy level for you?		
6. Do you feel pleased with your physical appearance?		
7. Are your drinking and eating habits healthy? (coffee, alcohol, cholesterol intake)		
8. Do you get adequate sleep?		
9. Is your stress at a healthy level?		
10. Do you take time for relaxation when necessary?		
11. Are your social activities conducive to good health?		
12. Do you seek to be in top physical condition, not using your age as an excuse?		
13. Do you take time to groom and dress well?		
14. Do you work in an environment that is conducive to good health?		

MY HEALTH/PHYSICAL GOALS

S _____

_____

_____

_____

M _____

_____

_____

_____

A _____

_____

_____

_____

R _____

_____

_____

_____

T _____

_____

_____

_____

Family

	YES	NO
1. Do you spend enough time with your family?		
2. Do you plan ahead for time with your family and close friends?		
3. Do you know each of your children well?		
4. Do you regularly celebrate special occasions with your spouse and family?		
5. Do you take time to make our spouse (or significant other) feel special and loved?		
6. Can your family count on you to meet their emotional needs? (To be there when needed?)		
7. Do you often express love to your family?		
8. Does your family feel safe, secure and comfortable?		
9. Do you really listen to your spouse and family when they need to talk to you?		
10. Are you positive and supportive toward your children and spouse?		
11. Can you leave your work stress at the office?		
12. Is your behavior with your family consistent?		
13. Can your children feel comfortable in bringing friends into your home?		
14. Have you planned for your family's financial needs?		

MY FAMILY GOALS

S _____

_____

_____

_____

M _____

_____

_____

_____

A _____

_____

_____

_____

R _____

_____

_____

_____

T _____

_____

_____

_____

Spiritual

	YES	NO
1. Do you allow enough time for relaxation and reflection?		
2. Do you include time for solitude on a daily basis?		
3. Do you have a clear idea about ethics and beliefs?		
4. Do you feel at peace with yourself, comfortable with who you are?		
5. Do you give your children ethical and spiritual training?		
6. Do you show acceptance of people who hold different religious/spiritual beliefs?		
7. Do your spiritual beliefs play an important role in your family unity?		
8. Is your work behavior consistent with your religious/spiritual beliefs?		
9. Are you able to say "no" when the situation requires it?		
10. Are your actions in business, in you family life and in social situations consistent with your spiritual beliefs?		

MY SPIRITUAL GOALS

S _____

_____

_____

_____

M _____

_____

_____

_____

A _____

_____

_____

_____

R _____

_____

_____

_____

T _____

_____

_____

_____

Intellectual/Personal Development

	YES	NO
1. Do you continuously seek opportunities for growth and learning?		
2. Do you write and creatively visualize goals on a daily basis?		
3. Do you feel satisfied with your knowledge level in your professional life?		
4. Do you try to extend your knowledge in areas that don't come naturally to you?		
5. Do you enjoy the challenge of the unknown?		
6. Do you feel your mind is as sharp as it has ever been?		
7. Does your life reflect the aspirations you have for yourself?		
8. Do you enjoy your work and find it fulfilling?		
9. Do you associate with people who stimulate you and who respect your viewpoints?		
10. Do you read journals and books that further your intellectual development?		
11. Have you taken outside courses in the past year?		
12. Do you follow current events in newspapers and on television?		
13. Are you aware of changing political, social, and economic trends in your environment?		
14. Do you take responsibility for you own intellectual/personal development needs?		
15. Do you like and respect yourself?		

MY INTELLECTUAL/PERSONAL GROWTH GOALS

S _____

_____

_____

_____

M _____

_____

_____

_____

A _____

_____

_____

_____

R _____

_____

_____

_____

T _____

_____

_____

_____

Community/Social

	YES	NO
1. Do you feel comfortable in and do you seek out social situations?		
2. Do you participate in community events?		
3. Are you able to make others feel at ease in social situations?		
4. Do you take the initiative to introduce yourself?		
5. Are you able to converse comfortably with a variety of different people?		
6. Can you rotate smoothly among conversations in a large group situation?		
7. Do you feel comfortable inviting business associates to your home?		
8. Do you look at people when you talk to them?		
9. Are you a good listener?		
10. Do you share eye contact with all the people with whom you are speaking, not just the socially important ones?		
11. Do you feel comfortable speaking in public?		
12. Do you go to great lengths to honour your commitments?		
13. Are you overly concerned about what others think of you?		
14. Are you able to persuade others and make them feel confident in you?		
15. Do you feel comfortable making introductions?		
16. Do you have a firm handshake?		
17. Do you remember people's names or things of importance to them?		

MY COMMUNITY/SOCIAL GOALS

S _____

_____

_____

_____

M _____

_____

_____

_____

A _____

_____

_____

_____

R _____

_____

_____

_____

T _____

_____

_____

_____

Work/Financial

	YES	NO
1. Do you spend quality time planning and scheduling your work activities?		
2. Do you prioritize your tasks?		
3. Do you follow your schedule most of the time? Are you effective in delegating tasks to others?		
4. Are you effective in delegating tasks to others?		
5. Are you able to stay focused and complete tasks you start?		
6. Are you able to be assertive when necessary?		
7. Do you keep up on trends and new information related to your work?		
8. Do you meet the commitments you set?		
9. Are you a positive force for others and a team player?		
10. Do you usually maintain a positive attitude toward your work?		
11. Do you get along well with all levels of staff in your organization?		
12. Do you return your phone calls promptly?		
13. Do you follow up on requests or commitments?		
14. Are you reliable and dependable?		
15. Are you able to work within your planned budget most of the time?		
16. Do you seek ongoing professional development?		
17. Do you take care of details?		
18. Do you generally use your work time well?		

WORK/FINANCIAL GOALS

S _____

_____

_____

_____

M _____

_____

_____

_____

A _____

_____

_____

_____

R _____

_____

_____

_____

T _____

_____

_____

_____

CHAPTER 12

Are we there yet?

Did you read your card today? Child like repetition is the key. You can do it! Child like persistence will really help. I have a question for you. Have you ever waited for a bus and walked away only to notice the bus pass by? Frustrating isn't it? One commonality of people who achieve their goals is that they are focused and persistent. Sometimes it's challenging to stay on track. That's why you want to focus on your card every day. In the event you miss a day you'll need to start over again. It's ok to fail, it's not ok to fail to try.

Sometimes you may lose your perspective in terms of failing. When you fail, you learn something. When you fail to try you learn not to try. You want to keep failing in perspective. This can be more difficult for some than others. Perfectionists, for example tend to avoid failure and impact others, often in a negative way.

My mother was a perfectionist and as a young man I wanted to make her happy. I remember when I started dating I'd bring females home seeking her approval. She found fault with every girl I brought home. They were too young or too old. They were too smart or not smart enough. They were too tall or too short.

No matter whom I brought home my mother found fault. I was frustrated. I wanted my mom to like the girls I was dating.

One day in my frustration I asked my older brother for some help. His suggestion to me was simple. Find a girl who is like mom. When she meets someone with a similar personality she'll like her. His plan seemed to make sense.

Then one day I met her. It was unbelievable how similar this girl was to my mother. She walked like my mother, she talked like my mother, she thought like my mother. Guess what? When I brought her home my father didn't like her. The moral of the story is simple. You can't please everyone and those seeking perfection are usually disappointed.

Remember the importance of positive self-talk (question #6) on your card. Imagine encouraging yourself as much as you encourage others. You need to make a decision. Are you for yourself or are you against yourself? There is no shortage of those who will put you or your dreams down. You're not one of them are you? When you choose to give yourself positive re-enforcement you will not be discouraged less easily.

Visualizing your goals daily (question #3) will help you stay focused and persistent. Remember to focus on positive outcomes. See and feel yourself benefiting from reaching your goals. Incorporate all your senses of sight, sound, smell, taste and touch. See yourself in the picture and feel the feelings. What you'll see is what you'll get.

It's also important to focus on positives. In the computer business there is a common phrase referred to as GIGO. This simply means garbage in-garbage out. In other words, if you put garbage into the computer which cannot distinguish between right and wrong it will store that data. All you'll get later is garbage out.

How about your computer? Your mind is the most powerful computer there is. You want to program your computer with good information so you get good information out. You achieve positive results when you focus on positives staying focused and persistent. Read this question every day as a positive reminder.

Key Question:

Am I focused and persistent?

MAGIC BULLETS

- Focus is a common trait in successful people.

- Setting written goals will increase your focus.

- Write down what is really important to you.

- Put good things in and you'll get good things out.

- Persistence pays off.

Prioritize

As you read your card each day you want to reflect on the ten attitudes. Some will be more relevant to you than others. It's time to prioritize so place a 1 beside the most important attitude a 2 beside the next most important and so on.

_____ putting thought into action

_____ setting S.M.A.R.T. goals

_____ visualizing your goals

_____ stretching your comfort zone

_____ appreciating what you have

_____ positive self-talk

_____ positive force for others

_____ actions consistent with values

_____ staying in balance

_____ focused and persistent

When you read your card daily you will spend more time on some attitudes than others. Prioritization is an important first step. Are you doing things right or are you doing the right things?

CHAPTER **13**

The most important lesson you will ever learn!

So here you are. Did you read your card today? Remember that's the plan. This is not a novel. The whole idea here is to put thought into action. That's the first question on your card you read three times daily. Great things come from simple beginnings. It may seem strange at first, as your comfort zone may have other ideas. Then, with repetition an increased awareness will take over you. You're filling your mind with positive thoughts and what you put in is what you'll get out. It is the implementation of the idea that is your challenge. Implementation then child like repetition will lead to your ultimate goal of internalization. Then everything becomes easier and you're having a lot more fun.

The Magic Bullet is not about sales yet it is. When you internalize the attitudes and practice the relevant skills you will sell more. This book is not about parenting skills yet it is. When you internalize the attitudes and practice the people skills you will parent better. Similarly it's not about customer service but service providers will serve better. It's not about management yet those who internalize the attitudes and skills will manage more effectively. As a matter of fact when you internalize the attitudes and relevant skills you'll be a better father, sister, brother, teacher and the list goes on.

When you adjust your attitude in a positive direction you feel better. When you feel better you think better. Thinking well in anything you do will cause you to act better. When you act better you create positive habits. When you create positive habits you achieve greater results. The idea here is to stay positively self motivated every day and learn to implement the most important skills first. It's the implementation of the simple things that matters. Common sense dictates that when you improve your attitude it will have a positive impact on all that you do.

This book is about the synergy created when you internalize positive attitudes on a daily basis and focus on relevant skills. The sum of the two is greater than the sum of the parts. I've written of positive attitudes that when implemented and ultimately internalized will lead to positive results.

I've referred to the term relevant skills for a reason. It's the implementation of the simple things that leads to greatness. A simple truth is that this skill applies to all of us. This skill is the most important one of all. When you apply this skill you will be better in all that you do. You will be a better parent, manager, salesperson, teacher, leader, server, coach. In short, internalizing this skill will improve everything.

This skill is the most important one there is. I will only write of this one skill in the book because this skill will impact all the others. Perhaps you are really good at this skill or perhaps there is much to improve. One thing is for sure you can always get better at it.

I write of one skill not with the intent of discarding the importance of others. There are many valuable skills to learn. For a parent, recognition and other parenting skills can be useful. A salesperson with planning, prospecting, and other relevant skills will sell more. A manager with improved coaching, communication and other relevant skills will be a better manager. A teacher with improved presentation and listening skills will teach better. What I am saying is that regardless of your situation the skill I will focus on is the most important one there is.

All these other skills are meaningless if you don't have the one of which I write. I've written and implemented programs on all of the above over the years. I've had the good fortune to travel many miles and meet tens of thousands of people. People skills are the most important skills to learn. If your goal is to improve, then focus on improving your people skills.

The first step to improving your people skills is to better understand others. You're a better parent when you understand your children. As a manger, you manage more effectively when you understand people. A salesperson sells more when she better understands her clients. A server serves better when he understands his customers. A teacher teaches better when she improves her ability to understand her students. A leader will lead better when he improves his ability to understand people. Chances are you interface with people every day so understanding others and how they process information makes sense.

Understanding people as many have discovered can be complex. Different personalities process and evaluate information differently. Different personalities are motivated in different ways. People will react differently to the same thing. When you understand how other personality's process information you better understand how they want to be communicated to. When you adjust to the personality style of others you communicate more effectively.

I love to tell stories at my seminars and workshops. I've found these stories relieve tension with humor and more importantly help people remember the message. It's a great way to drive home a key point. I hope you see the humor but more importantly remember the message so please read carefully. To tell you the story, I need to take you many miles away...

It's a bright sunny day in Paris. At the train station people are busily about their day. One train bound for Vienna sits by the track as four travelers prepare to board the train. The long journey will soon begin.

The first person to walk into the compartment of the train is a general. The sun reflects off his polished brass as he walks briskly and purposely towards his seat. The general, like all of us has strengths and weaknesses that are part of his personality. Focusing on the positives first, the general is focused and driven to succeed. You can feel his intensity and drive. He is results oriented and will follow through with his determination to get the job done. The general is time conscious and likes to get to the point. His motto is, "Where's the beef?" He is a man of few words and has eyes that seem to look through you. The general, like all of us, has strengths and weaknesses. The general's greatest strength is his direct style. For purpose of illustration I'll describe the general's personality style as a Director. Remember that name as the train ride soon begins.

The next person to enter the train is a soldier. As he strides into the train you can feel his confidence. The soldier loves people and flashes his smile for all to see. Unlike the general, the soldier seems to have all the time in the world. The general may say few words but the soldier makes up for it. The soldier loves to talk. He loves to meet people. The soldier likes to have fun!

The soldier has strengths and weaknesses. This fellow has a charming quality and people love to be around him. He makes people feel good with his confident manner and smooth wit. Focusing on the strengths the soldier has the ability to easily socialize with others so I'll refer to him as a Socializer. Remember this name as well.

The third character walks into the train compartment trying hard not to be noticed. She is easily noticed as her beauty is undeniable. Her good looks go well beyond what you see on the outside. It's strange when you meet someone who initially looks good to you and then you get to know them. As you discover their personality they start looking better or worse to you based on what you discover on the inside. This can cause a metamorphosis as to how they look to you. Personality can make a person more or less beautiful in the eyes of the beholder.

The good news about this young lady is that she is kind, sincere and caring. She values relationships and gathers friends like flowers. She is sensitive to the feelings of others. This young woman puts the needs of others above her own. She like all of us has strengths and weaknesses. Focusing on her strengths she has a natural ability to relate to others. As a result, I'll refer to our third character, the young beautiful women as a Relater. Remember this name as well.

The last character to walk onto the train is an elderly woman. She cautiously walks in paying close attention to all around her. She places her luggage down methodically and sets out to organize for the trip. Map in hand, she plans to mark each and every station along the way. Always analyzing the situation she pays close attention to detail, planning to avoid surprises. She doesn't like surprises. This elderly woman like all of us has strengths and weaknesses. Her analytical skills and attention to detail shows how she thinks about things so I'll describe our last character, the elderly woman as a Thinker. Remember this name as well.

The train blows its whistle. Four different people can react differently to the same thing. The train rolls out of the station and there sit our four characters. The general, our Director with his strong posture looks straight ahead. He glances down at his watch already disturbed he will be late. The soldier, our Socializer glances around the train smiling trying to make eye contact with everyone, especially the young lady. The young lady, our Relater sits quietly. The elderly woman our Thinker sits there, her mind racing, going through her checklist of things to be done.

About an hour into the train ride and the sun is still shining. Up ahead is a long, dark tunnel. As the train enters the tunnel the four in the compartment soon sit in darkness. They move along in dark silence that seems like an eternity. Suddenly, in the train, in the darkness, in the tunnel you hear two distinct sounds. A kiss is followed by a thundering smack. You wonder what's going through their minds in the darkness, in the train, in the tunnel.

Moments later the train climbs out of the darkness back into the glorious sunshine. There sits the general, our Director with a red welt on his face. Everyone's mind in the train begins to race but none faster that the elderly woman, our Thinker. Her self-talk races and she thinks to herself, "good for that young lady, that general has the nerve to kiss her in the dark and she slaps his face. That's exactly what he deserves." The train ride continues.

The young woman, our Relater is considering things as well. "Why would that general wait all that time and then try to kiss the old lady and not me?" This seemed very strange to her. The train ride continues and the general, our Director thinks to himself, "is that soldier ever lucky he kisses that young girl and I get slapped." The soldier, our Socializer sits there with a broad grin on his face looking like the cat that ate the canary. He thinks to himself "am I ever smart? I kiss my hand, slap that general and no one knows a darn thing about it". Four different personalities react differently to the same thing.

MAGIC BULLETS

- Implementation then child like repetition will lead you to your goals.

- Your attitude will affect all areas of your life.

- There is a synergy created with attitudes and skills.

- People process information differently.

- Flexibility and being able to adjust is your key to success.

CHAPTER 14

Who are you?

Four different personalities react differently to the same experience. So who are you? Are you the outgoing Socializer? Could you be the intense, driven Director? Perhaps you are the sensitive Relater? Last but not least you may be an analytical Thinker. I'm sure that you have some of the characteristics of all these personality types but one is more dominant than the others.

There is no right or wrong personality style. Personalities are born and not made. The greatest change I've experienced in my life was having children. Learning from children as they grow is the greatest lesson of all. Every adult needs a child to teach for it is the way adults learn.

I remember before the kids came along I believed that environment and condition played the most influential role in determining personalities. Then I had children and soon realized that personalities were born and not made. It is interesting to me often how children from the same parents, living in the same home, and with the same values can be so different. I'm sure you have met parents who would describe the differences to you. Perhaps you have experienced this in your family.

I have three children with my eldest being my only girl, Laura. When Laura was born my life changed forever. As I watched my baby grow it didn't take long for Laura's personality to shine through. Laura is a Thinker who pays close attention to detail. Methodical by nature my wife and I referred to her as the, 'What if?' girl. She would calculate times between meals fearful of missing one or not being on time. When told of going for a car ride the questions would begin, "What if the car breaks down?" "It's ok Laura we'll walk to a gas station," we would reply. "What if we get lost?" she'd ask. "We'll stop and ask for directions," we would answer back. "What if I need to use the washroom? "We'll find you a washroom," I would repeat back to her. "What if I get hungry?" she would ask next. I would answer back, "We have snacks packed and we can buy some lunch." Laura did not like surprises, always needed a back up and always did her homework. Laura paid attention to detail. She still does today.

A couple of years later along came my boy. I assumed I was in for more of the same from Gary, based largely on my experience with Laura. There was another lesson to learn. Was I in for a surprise! Unlike Laura who was cautious by nature, Gary was the exact opposite, an outgoing social butterfly. He'd confidently place orders at restaurants and jump into deep ends of swimming pools. Where the order of things meant everything to my Thinker Laura, it meant nothing to my Socializer Gary. He was fearless by nature always charging forward seeking the next surprise. This is exactly how he is today.

Many years later along came our little surprise, another boy. As Cody began to grow his personality traits began to show. Cody is a Director. Focused and competitive Cody developed an early love for sports. Although he has a natural gift it is his ability to practice relentlessly that makes the biggest difference. He is driven to succeed and will practice to improve or learn a new skill over and over again. He is quietly competitive always seeking to improve. I've never had to ask or remind him to practice. It's in his nature to compete and excel and that is exactly how he is today.

Personalities are born and not made. Personalities will not change. Perhaps you have felt the sting of frustration when you've tried to change someone else. Since you can't change a personality it makes sense to understand it. One of the most important people skills to develop is expertise in understanding each personality style. When you understand another's personality style you can make adjustments and make it easier to be understood. This is not about manipulating others. It is about communicating to others in a manner that is understood.

You have a dominant personality style as well. Your style like others has strengths and potential weaknesses. Your challenge is that not everyone thinks as you do. Your other challenge is that they never will. Your ability to adjust to the personality style of others will increase your flexibility. You begin to better understand the personality traits of others, when you first understand your own.

The following exercise is not a test. I suggest you circle the questions with a pencil. Take your time and read the instructions.

There are a total of 88 questions designed to interpret your personality style using numerical examples. The four I will use to describe the four personality styles are those in our train ride. The Socializer, Director, Relater and Thinker are names to describe the inherent strength of each style.

The numbers you will add up later will indicate balance or an extreme example of a personality style. When your numbers are close more flexibility is indicated. Once you have a lock on your dominant style we will further explore strengths and potential weaknesses of your style.

I write potential weaknesses as this does not apply to everyone. Socializers, for example are notorious for being late but that does not apply to all of them. Directors are considered to be stubborn by nature but that does not apply to every Director. Relaters are considered to be too sensitive but not all are. Thinkers suffer from analysis paralysis but not all do. In other words generally speaking certain personalities have characteristics in common.

The purpose of this exercise is simple. The first step to better understanding others is to first better understand you. This way you can focus on your strengths and minimize or eliminate the weaknesses. Later on you'll develop a written action plan for those areas you want to focus on improving or changing.

EXERCISE: Personality Styles

This exercise is to help you (1) diagnose your own primary personality style and (2) identify ways in which you could modify your behavior when dealing with other people.

There are no wrong or right answers on this questionnaire. Your personal responses to the hypothetical situations in the exercise will be entirely unique.

Each self-descriptive statement is followed by four possible endings. In the lines to the right of each set of endings, please print the numeral 6 next to the ending that is most like you. Now print a 4 besides the ending that is next to being most like you. A 3 goes next to the ending that comes in third. The ending that is least like you will rate a 1.

6 = most like you;

4 = next most like you;

3 = next most;

1 = least most

Example

When I am challenged to resolve a negative situation, I usually:

1. can generate many ideas to alleviate the problem. _____

2. focus on the outcomes of possible solutions. (least like me) _____

3. determine what happened before the _____

4. problems and analyze the facts. (most like me) _____

5. listen to my feelings about the situation. _____

QUESTIONNAIRE

In my daily life, I may become preoccupied with:

1. intellectual sparring, to keep my wits agile. _____

2. maintaining good relationships with others. _____

3. getting the best results possible for today. _____

4. the dream world of incubating ideas and concepts. _____

When talking to other people, I often will:

1. wander off mentally when the subject gets too detailed _____

2. becomes disinterested in concepts which lack originality _____

3. be somewhat indirect and avoid confrontation. _____

4. show irritation with those who are not fully prepared. _____

When communicating my concern regarding a problem, I try to:

1. state the facts and find a mutually acceptable solution. _____

2. outline the history of the situation, linking past events with the current problem. _____

3. concisely list the actions that the other party must take in order to alleviate the situation. _____

4. include my personal feelings and touch on the positive aspects of the situation. _____

In stressful situations, I may sometimes:

1. become very assertive and seek control of the outcome. _____

2. move at a studied pace and perhaps miss opportunities which could have proved useful. _____

3. get talked into something by others in order to preserve harmony. _____

4. spontaneously express my feelings, later wishing I was less candid. _____

I feel a great sense of accomplishment when I:

1. achieve more goals than I had anticipated. _____

2. sense the true feelings of others, helping them where possible. _____

3. find the answer through careful analysis of all available data. _____

4. create new approaches and concepts which will be appreciated by other people. _____

In going about my daily tasks, people would describe me as:

1. relaxed and easy going. _____

2. careful and analytical. _____

3. quick and decisive. _____

4. fast and spontaneous. _____

It would bother me greatly to be viewed by colleagues as:

1. over my head. _____

2. lazy and disorganized. _____

3. confrontational and self-serving. _____

4. insignificant and ready to be put "out to pasture". _____

When discussing ideas with people who hold different views, I aid the conversation by:

1. being flexible and working toward "common ground". _____

2. keeping calm while guiding the others to logically understand all the details. _____

3. using my conceptual abilities in order to unite the various aspects of the situation. _____

4. "trading places" in my imagination with the other side, in order to understand the emotions involved. _____

When working with other people I tend to:

1. systematically develop tasks in a logical order. _____

2. be relaxed, friendly and informal. _____

3. measure tasks against the time and money necessary to do a good job. _____

4. want to be appreciated for my creativity and ideas. _____

When making a first acquaintance, I usually try to:

1. keep to my usual approach, since it has worked before. _____

2. let them know about my creative talents. _____

3. say whatever comes off the top of my head, without worrying how they may take it. _____

4. concentrate on helping them to feel at ease with me. _____

At my worst, I can be:

1. too pushy and competitive. _____

2. too impulsive and, at times, noncommittal. _____

3. too outgoing and direct. _____

4. too detail-oriented and self-contained. _____

When I feel I am under pressure, I tend to:

1. react immediately, swept off by the tide of my emotions. _____

2. give in to others too quickly. _____

3. retreat to a position where I can put things in "proper perspective". _____

4. take action to ensure I retain control. _____

When dealing with people with whom I have infrequent contact, I hope I am seen as:

1. a bright and enthusiastic person who understands other people's feelings and needs. _____

2. a bottom-line oriented individual who could lead people to make the right decision to achieve the goal. _____

3. a sensitive, supportive person who is a team player. _____

4. a detail-oriented individual who can analyze any difficulties people are facing. _____

When faced with challenges in achieving my goals, I try to:

1. understand the actions of people who stand in my way and view the "big picture". _____

2. quickly review how others are achieving results and develop a team plan to accomplish the objective. _____

3. identify the major hurdle and establish the most efficient way to overcome it. _____

4. review the events and define an intelligent, organized approach. _____

Key priorities for me in my work are:

1. managing my workload effectively and completing tasks. _____

2. ensuring that the desired bottom-line results of the team are being achieved. _____

3. building relationships with my colleagues, customers and key suppliers. _____

4. keeping the work group challenged and focused on a shared vision. _____

I must be conscious of my actions because people Could feel that I am:

1. too independent, competitive, and single-minded. _____

2. excitable, unorganized, and talkative. _____

3. cautious, and non-confrontational. _____

4. predictable, structured, and slow. _____

I like to be around other people who are:

1. friendly and interesting. _____

2. comfortable to be around. _____

3. competent and seem to be accomplishing goals. _____

4. contemplative and non-intrusive. _____

I find it easiest to influence others when I am:

1. outgoing and optimistic. _____

2. aware of the underlying emotions being felt by all concerned. _____

3. being concise and direct. _____

4. patient, prepared and logical. _____

I become most irritated by people who are:

1. unpredictable and out of control. _____

2. inefficient and indecisive. _____

3. inflexible and guided by routine. _____

4. impatient and insensitive to the feelings of others. _____

People would probably describe my work space as:

1. relaxed and comfortable. _____

2. cluttered, personal and friendly. _____

3. busy, efficient and formal. _____

4. organized, functional and businesslike. _____

When making an important buying decision, I primarily consider:

1. how others will react. _____

2. the personal benefits it will bring. _____

3. what it should accomplish and at what cost. _____

4. what information is available to support
   its relevance to my needs. _____

My preferred work situation is one where I:

1. am in charge and empowered to make crucial decisions. _____

2. have the opportunity and to make an important
   contribution to organizational goals. _____

3. can work relatively independently and be
   accountable for my work. _____

4. have ample opportunity for social
   interaction with others. _____

DIRECTIONS FOR SCORING:

The scoring sheet is divided into two sections: (1) normal conditions and (2) stress conditions. It is interesting to see our behavioral style when we're under pressure, as often we act differently under stress.

1. You will find it most convenient to enter your responses sequentially from 1 to 88.

2. Enter the response value (6, 4, 3, or 1) to the right of each corresponding response number. You should have a response value for every box on the scoring sheet.

3. Total the scores for "Normal" Conditions by assign the columns vertically. You should have a Total Score for each of the four columns, S, D, T, and R.

4. Check your totals by adding horizontally the four Total Scores. It should equal

5. Now total the scores for "Stress" Conditions by adding the columns vertically. Again, you should have a Total Score for each of the four columns, S, D, T, and R.

6. Check your totals by adding the four Total Scores horizontally. Again, it should equal 154.

7. Note which columns show the highest score for you.

S = Socializer

D = Director

T = Thinker

R = Relater

This reflects your primary behavioral style under "normal" conditions and under "stress" conditions.

No style is superior or inferior. People use different behavioral styles in different situations. The key in behavioral flexibility is to recognize your own dominant style so that you can prepare to adjust to others.

SCORING SHEET
Behavioral Flexibility

"NORMAL" CONDITIONS

S		D		T		R		
RESPONSE	SCORE	RESPONSE	SCORE	RESPONSE	SCORE	RESPONSE	SCORE	
4		3		1		2		
6		5		8		7		
20		17		19		18		
24		23		22		21		TOTAL
28		25		26		27		SCORE
36		35		33		34		
60		58		57		59		
65		67		68		66		
69		71		72		70		
78		79		80		77		
88		85		87		86		
TOTAL								TOTAL

"STRESS" CONDITIONS

S		D		T		R		
RESPONSE	SCORE	RESPONSE	SCORE	RESPONSE	SCORE	RESPONSE	SCORE	
12		11		10		9		
16		13		14		15		
32		31		30		29		
38		39		37		40		
43		41		44		42		**TOTAL**
45		48		47		46		**SCORE**
49		50		52		51		
53		55		56		54		
62		61		64		63		
75		74		73		76		
82		83		84		81		
TOTAL								**TOTAL**

MAGIC BULLETS

- Four different personality styles will react differently to the same thing.

- There is no wrong or right personality style.

- You have the dominant personality style and so do others.

- Many personality styles adjust under stress.

- Each personality style has strengths and weaknesses.

CHAPTER 15

It all adds up!

Your numbers illustrate your dominant personality style and to what degree. When your numbers are close this indicates flexibility. In addition, the numbers in the lower box refer to how you act under stress. Some behaviors magnify or change under stress. I'm sure you've heard or read of the importance of understanding personality styles. You may have heard different personalities described as analyzers, promoters or drivers. Perhaps you've had these styles described by colors or animals. The names may change but the game stays the same.

The internalization of this skill is your ultimate objective. Your value will increase when you do so. Internalization is always a challenge. You want to master this skill. Do you remember your first question on your card? Am I putting thought into action? Putting thought into action is only the beginning. Implementation is the starting point but internalization is the ultimate goal. It will take time, effort and child like repetition to internalize this important skill.

There are learning stages to be aware of. Your goal here is not to simply read but apply. Then you will experience value.

Your goal is to focus on your attitude. Did you read your card today? This is your life. You need to be acutely aware, studying people as you grow. Regardless of your chosen field everything improves when this skill improves. Your ultimate goal is internalization, making it part of you, an automatic response if you will. I want to remind or make you aware of the stages you will go through to reach the ultimate goal of internalization. I hope you can relate to my story...

Earlier I wrote of the sub-conscious mind and how you can see clearly and feel an experience that may have happened many years ago. It seems like some of these experiences happened yesterday. Do you remember your first car? Do you remember the color, the upholstery, the gear shift? I bought my first car, a used blue Volkswagen one month before getting my driver's license. My big brother brought it home. I had been practicing on my dad's automatic and hadn't driven a standard. I did watch my brother carefully when he drove my car home and parked it. There sat my car in the driveway waiting for me to drive it. Days that seemed like weeks passed and my anticipation grew.

I had practiced with my father's car for months and thought the smaller Volkswagen would be easier to drive. I could hardly wait to drive my new car without my father watching me. One day, I couldn't wait any longer and seeing my car at the top of our long driveway was a temptation I couldn't resist. I didn't have my license yet but as I said it was a long driveway. My dad was really strict but as you know, parents seem less strict when they're not there. I seized a quiet moment one day and I grabbed the keys anxious to try my car.

I sat in the car and made myself comfortable. It was smaller and I noticed it had one extra pedal. That was the pedal my brother Wayne kept pushing in and out when he drove the car home. Please understand I'm a city boy and hadn't been exposed to machinery in my life. I was at the first stage of learning, unconscious incompetence. I didn't know that I didn't know. I was about to find out.

I put the keys in the ignition and turned the key. My heart raced when the car leapt forward like a frog on a pond. Worse still the car kept hopping and bouncing down the driveway. Finally I got it to stop. The car had moved and surely my father would notice. Yeah he'd notice! What would I do? In that moment of frustration and paranoia my brother arrived home. Needless to say, I was glad to see him. I realized at that point that I needed help to learn how to drive the car. I had gone from being unconsciously incompetent to becoming consciously incompetent. I knew that I didn't know how to drive that car and I needed help.

My brother explained how a manual transmission worked. He showed me the clutch and explained what it did. We sat in the car and he walked through how you need to push the clutch down and put the car in first gear. Then he said, "As you release the clutch, you give it a little more gas and you're off and running." It sure sounded easy. It wasn't quite that easy at first. Was it that easy for you? I have vivid memories of bouncing along our driveway at first and then later when I had my license, terrorizing the streets.

When I finally got the car moving, my brother coached me and suggested I shift from first to second gear. Once again, it wasn't quite as easy as he had explained. I can still hear those gears grinding. Gradually though day-by-day, shifting gears became easier and the ride became smoother. I found that I really had to concentrate on that clutch. Timing was everything. I started disliking hills but after a while and a few panic attacks that became easier as well. I was at the third learning stage, conscious competence. In other words, I knew how to shift gears and work the clutch but I had to really concentrate on every step. I was consciously competent.

Then the magic day arrived. I was driving along the road shifting the gears, working the clutch with ease. I didn't have to think about it. It's the same feeling you get when learning to play an instrument or learning a new language. You don't have to think about it, you just do it. I couldn't stall the vehicle it seemed even if I wanted to. I found myself shifting gears without thought. Driving a standard had become an automatic response. I had reached the ultimate fourth step of Unconscious competence. I could do it without thinking about it. I had internalized the skill. This is a wonderful place to be for there is a lot less friction.

You may drive, or have driven a vehicle with a manual transmission. You learned to shift gears by choice or necessity. When you had to drive every day, a lifetime habit was created. This habit may take a week or a month but like riding a bike, it's a habit for life. You want to get around and are forced to practice daily. As a result you internalize the skill. Learning and applying a new skill becomes an automated response over time. Performing the task with ease reduces friction. Think of how improving people skills will reduce friction for you.

MAGIC BULLETS

- The highest number indicate you dominant personality style.

- The lowest number indicates your biggest challenge.

- Internalize seen the ability to read personality styles is the key to building rapport.

- There are learning stages you must pass through.

- Practice makes permanent.

CHAPTER 16

It begins with understanding

Understanding personality styles is an important people skill that, when internalized will impact all areas of your life. There are four dominant personality styles. Although different names have been chosen to describe the four styles the process in determining a dominant style remains the same.

On the next page there is a vertical line. At the top of the line are open and at the bottom are closed behaviors. Each personality style has predictable behaviors. Open and closed behaviors help to define a characteristic of a personality. The more open a person is the more easily they show their emotions. People who exhibit open behaviors wear their hearts on their sleeves. When people with open behaviors get excited they get excited. You may say that they are not the best poker players. Open people tend to be extroverts, speaking demonstratively with facial expressions and hand movement. Happy or sad, a smile or a frown, a warm handshake it's easy to identify people with open behaviors.

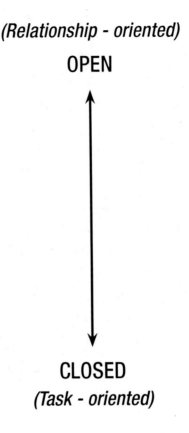

(Relationship - oriented)

OPEN

CLOSED

(Task - oriented)

At the bottom of the line you see the word closed. People who exhibit closed behaviors are the opposite of open behaviors. The more closed a person is the less they show their emotions. People with closed behaviors don't show their feelings easily. Whether these people are happy or sad, mad or scared it's hard to tell. Closed people tend to be more introverted, speaking purposely with minimal gestures and hand movement. Closed people tend to be more difficult to read as they play their hands close to their chest. Closed people speak purposefully and are less animated.

The openness scale applies to everyone differently as it's a matter of degrees. Some people are more open than others and some are more closed. If for example a 10 is at the top of the scale representing how open you are and a 1 at the bottom represented how closed you are, you would be somewhere on this scale.

Below is a horizontal line. This line is the directness scale. On the right you see direct behaviors and on the left indirect behaviors. The directness scale refers to what degree of control your personality exhibits. Some people want to be in charge and some don't. Perhaps you want to drive the bus. Perhaps you want to ride it. People with direct behaviors are assertive, take charge people who like to be in control. They make decisions quickly often based on gut feelings of trust.

INDIRECT ⟵⟶ DIRECT

Those who exhibit indirect behaviors are less assertive and take longer to make decisions. Indirect people are more information driven. They pay more attention to details. Indirect people are more process driven and cautious. They don't want to be the centre of attention.

The directness scale applies to you. You are somewhere on the directness scale. Some people are more direct than others and others are less. The directness scale helps you to identify the dominant personality style of others.

As you can see in the illustration below, when you cross the openness scale and the directness scale there are quadrants. These quadrants illustrate the four dominant personality styles. As stated earlier many have used different descriptive names to describe each personality style but the process remains the same. Each of these four personality styles has unique characteristics. The Socializer, Director, Relater and Thinker are the four descriptive names. The names chosen based on the natural strength of each style. Let's examine each personality style in relation to the openness and directness scale.

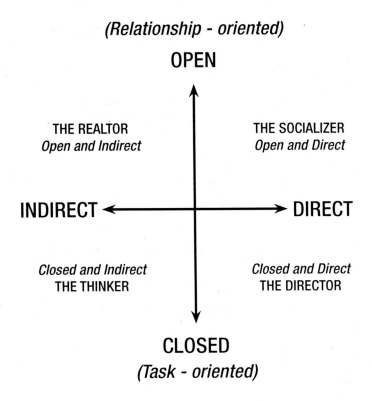

(Relationship - oriented)
OPEN

THE REALTOR
Open and Indirect

THE SOCIALIZER
Open and Direct

INDIRECT ← → **DIRECT**

Closed and Indirect
THE THINKER

Closed and Direct
THE DIRECTOR

CLOSED
(Task - oriented)

At the top right of the quadrant is the Socializer. As a Socializer you are open and direct. Your openness makes you an extrovert who loves meeting people. Your directness makes you a spontaneous person who makes decisions quickly often with ease. If it feels right and trust is high you will do it. People love your energy and spontaneous nature. You have a good sense of humor. You like to make people laugh. People often meet with you for an hour, talk of nothing specific and leave feeling good anyway. You are quick on your feet and easily turn on the charm. You have energy to burn. Where did you get all that energy from? You are at ease with people and establish rapport easily. You're not afraid of the limelight rather you enjoy it. You may dress accordingly often wearing brighter colors. How you dress is important to you. Your clothes, along with your strong posture are a winning combination. Where is that red sports car you want? You have great Social skills.

The Socializer has much strength with the ability to socialize easily with others. As a Socializer you also have potential weaknesses. I write potential because as discussed earlier, these weaknesses will not always apply to each personality. I suggest if the weakness applies to you then make a mental note. Later you will develop and prioritize an action plan to improve.

Socializers love to talk and often this inhibits their ability to listen. To a Socializer time is meaningless and many make unrealistic time estimates. This is why Socializers are often late. Socializers are not good at paying attention to detail. Socializers like the big picture and not the little steps to get there. Socializers speak of goals; they visualize goals but hardly ever write them down. Written goals work best. Socializers often fly by the seat of their pants often stressing others and not themselves. Socializers resist structure as they believe that structure inhibits their freedom. Structure brings freedom.

At the bottom right of the quadrant is the Director. As a Director you are closed and direct. Your closed nature makes you hard to read as you don't show your feelings easily. You share the characteristic of directness with the Socializer. You too make decisions quickly and with ease but for a different reason. You know what you want. You are intense, focused on your goals and you are conscious of time. You want to use your time wisely. You don't like to waste it. How did you get so competitive? You are results oriented and focus on the bottom line.

You can intimidate others and not know that you are doing so. You don't appreciate small talk. You are direct and like to get to the point. Your motto is, "Where's the beef?" The limelight is ok but it's the results that get you excited. You like to plan, implement and measure results. You are a fearless warrior destined to conquer. Forget about the red sports car, you want something big and dark. How about a Sherman tank? You know something you could blow the other cars away that are in your way. You prefer to wear dark, conservative colors. Power suits were created for Directors.

As a Director you have much strength. You have potential weaknesses as well. Your opinions are so strong that they can often be offensive to other people, not that you care that much. You easily forget that others have feelings and not everyone is like you. You can be stubborn and inflexible. You are like a juggler, a control freak who can't let go. Often when you do let go you explode. Any anger management problems? Are you stressed out? Often Directors become paranoid and sometimes they crash.

Sometimes others see you as a bully totally insensitive to the needs of others. They see you as totally focused on your goals and unaware of the feelings of others. I've worked with many Directors in my life. Directors with people skills are a powerful force. These people make great leaders. Directors lacking people skills are your worst nightmare. These individuals sadly never reach their true potential.

At the bottom left is the Thinker. As a Thinker you are closed like the Director. Unlike the Director you are indirect. Your closed nature makes you more of an introvert. It takes you more time to get comfortable with people. You don't want to be in the limelight in fact, you'll avoid it. Your indirect behavior results in being more process oriented. You are information driven and you plan ahead paying close attention to all the steps.

You're punctual, reliable and get things done on time. You like routine. You wash your car and have it serviced on time. You even have the receipts for repairs. You are a great person to buy a used car from. You're information driven and want the facts before making a decision. As a result it takes you longer to make decisions. You believe that you make better decisions as a result. You have excellent planning skills and pay close attention to details. As a result you are a reliable, dependable person who thinks before you speak. Forget about that big car. Forget about the sex appeal of a sports car. You want a vehicle that is fuel efficient with a good re-sale value. You are practical. You think ahead.

Thinkers have potential weaknesses as well. Thinkers have restricted comfort zones. As discussed in the attitudinal portion earlier we all have a comfort zone that acts as a regulating system. Focus on question four on your card. Am I stretching my comfort zone? Your comfort zone is more narrow than most. You are a creature of habit and these habits can lead to ruts. Thinkers also have a tendency towards perfectionism. This is tough when you live in an imperfect world. You may suffer from analysis paralysis and get too hung up on details. You think when I get it right, have all the details, no gray areas then you'll take action. In the meantime life can pass you by. Do one or two typo errors take you off track? Think about it!

At the top left is the Relater. As a Relater you are open and indirect. The openness of your personality shines through. An open and warm personality you are an empathetic sponge for others. You care about people and tune in easily to their feelings. When someone needs a shoulder to cry on they usually find yours. You're a great listener. You make a great friend. You put the feelings of the others before your own. How do you tune in to the feelings of others so easily? People feel so comfortable around you. You are a great team player as you relate so well with others. The indirect nature of your personality makes you more cautious than the Socializer.

You are more security oriented and are not prone to gamble. You don't like slick or aggressive people and feel pressured easily by them. Fast talkers and loud people turn you off. You have a hard time understanding how many people are so insensitive to the needs of others. Forget about the cars, where is your brown minivan? You can drive that team around or help a friend. You relate well with other people.

Relaters have potential weaknesses as well. Your ability to tune into the feelings of others can have negative affects. You may internalize the feelings of others so much that you lose yourself. You also have difficulty saying no. This can manifest itself in time management problems. You believe that you are not assertive enough and perhaps give in too easily. You have difficulty accepting criticism even if it is constructive and properly presented. You burn on emotion and as a result are prone to highs and lows more often than others. Sometimes you are so descriptive that it takes you forever to get to your point driving Directors crazy everywhere.

MAGIC BULLETS

- Understanding personality styles will have a positive impact on all areas of your life.

- Open behaviours indicate how easily someone "shows emotion or reaction.

- Closed behaviours indicate a lack of emotion or expression.

- Direct behaviours indicate that a person wants to be in control.

- Indirect behaviours indicates a lack of need for control and the decision making process.

CHAPTER 17

Will you adjust?

As I write descriptions of each personality, you may think that you have some of the characteristics of each personality described. You probably do. There is; however, your dominant style. Your personality was born not made. You process information differently than the other personality styles. What is important to you is not important to them. Others are motivated differently than you. Your personality will not change. The personality of others won't change either. Many have suffered the consequences of trying to change someone else's personality. You can't do it and you'll frustrate yourself in the process.

Frustration manifests itself in many ways. Parents struggle to get through to a child; a manger attempts to manage a situation; a salesperson wants to make a sale; a couple tries to understand each other. If only everyone you met was just like you. When you do meet this person just like you there is instant rapport. You think the same and have so much in common. That's easy but how about those other three personalities? You want to be flexible so you can relate to them as well. You want to build rapport with them too?

Have you ever met someone where there was no rapport established? You couldn't put you finger on why but you just don't like that person. You may have experienced a personality conflict with someone else. There is a reason for this. You are exact opposites. You know when they see black, you see white, when they say left, you say right. You feel uncomfortable tension when this person is around. It can be unbearable to be in the same room.

The personality style that doesn't share any of our characteristics is a direct opposite to you. These personalities can present challenges for you as they process information totally differently than you do. You'll need to make your biggest adjustments with these people. Remember their personality will not change. You want to master how to identify and adjust to their personality. You want to understand it. This way you can manage tension, build rapport and communicate more effectively.

Take a look at the personality directly opposite to yours. Socializers and Directors share directness. Thinkers and Relaters are both indirect. At least there are some things in common. On the other hand, Directors and Relaters and Socializers and Thinkers have nothing in common. If you are a Socializer beware of those Thinkers. If you are a Thinker beware of those Socializers. You are direct opposites. For you Directors watch out for those Relaters. For you Relaters watch out for those Directors. You are direct opposites as well.

Here is an example of conflicting personalities and what can happen when two people don't adjust. I read recently that those who marry today have as much chance of separating as they do staying together. Needless to say, in this world we live in the divorce rates are high. People for a variety of reasons go their separate ways and many lives are affected. It's interesting how opposites attract. They attract it seems but frequently don't stay together. There must be a reason for this. In this example a Director and a Relater meet.

The Director is a successful business woman. She is driven to succeed. Like a juggler she maintains control of her growing empire. Her energy and drive to succeed propels her forward. She knows what she wants and it's best not to get in her way. She has her eyes on the prize. Many people admire her sheer will and determination. She's results oriented and gets it done with intensity and perseverance.

Although others admire her, she admires others. She has difficulty warming up to people. Sometimes she offends them. She sees others as social butterflies that seemed loved by all. I wish I had that magic, she thinks. Like most of us she takes her own gifts for granted and admires the gifts of others.

The Relater is a gentle person. He cares about other people. He has gathered friends like flowers and relationships are his highest priority. His people skills and ability to empathize with others develops instant rapport. People love to be around him. A kind, caring person, others admire his ability to relate well with others. Although others admire him he too admires others. I wish I was more assertive, he thinks? I have to learn to say no, he thinks. He believes that he's not tough enough and let's people walk all over him. Sometimes he feels used.

One day the two meet. The Relater, who believes he isn't focused enough, meets someone focused and driven to succeed. He admires the way she stands up and takes tough stands. No one walks over her. She knows how to say no! She knows where she's going and people don't push her around. When she doesn't like the meal served, she sends it back. He likes the fact that she knows what she wants. An attraction is formed.

The Director admires the people skills of the Relater. People just love to be around him. She sees he is relaxed and not totally focused on time. She finds it soothing to be around him. I'd like people to warm up to me like that, she thinks. She loves the way he puts her feelings first. From a personality perspective an attraction is formed.

Over time, each personality reveals itself in a variety of situations. These two personalities were born not made. Once again, you can't change personality so what's important is to understand it. One day, the Relater watches the Director criticize someone in public. Someone has made the mistake of crossing her path. How can she be so insensitive, he thinks? Her drive and intensity he found so attractive causes her to often work late. Why is work so important, he wonders? If only I were more important to her than her career. He wishes she was a little less intense.

One day, the Director watches the Relater struggle over a decision. What's wrong with this wimp, she thinks, can't he make a decision? Decisions are so easy for her to make. Another time she wants to rush him away. Time is so precious, why is he is so slow, she thinks? It takes him so long to get to the point, she thinks. Doesn't he recognize the importance of my schedule and reaching my goals? Over time friction builds. What seemed attractive begins to lose the attraction. The Relater thrives on emotional support. The Director doesn't know what emotional support is. The seeds of dissent begin to grow.

Here is another potential conflict between two other direct opposites, the Socializer and the Thinker. The Socializer is a salesperson and the Thinker is a business owner. The Socializer has been a salesperson for five years. Although there have been ups and downs, the Socializer's attitude always shines through. She loves meeting people and people love to be around her. She's quick on her feet, has a great sense of humor and a good command of language. She'll talk your ear off, if you let her and she loves to engage in small talk. She relies on her personality and charm to succeed in sales. She relies less on research, facts and pays little attention to detail. Soon she will make a presentation to a Thinker.

The Thinker has operated his business successfully for ten years. There have been few ups or downs in the business as he plans ahead. He prefers to be in the background utilizing his planning skills and analyzing every potential outcome. He doesn't feel comfortable around people and is generally suspicious of others, especially fast, smooth talkers.

He is methodical and likes to pay attention to all the details. He loves to analyze information comparing products and services. It takes him longer to make decisions, but he feels confident that he makes better ones as a result. He doesn't like loud, aggressive, or manipulative people and it takes him longer to develop rapport. Soon the Socializer will arrive at his office for an initial meeting.

When the salesperson arrives she is late. Socializers can be late. Time is not that important to her anyway. It is important to him. Not a good way to start a meeting. The salesperson flashes her bright smile and launches into her presentation. Socializers love to talk and often too quickly. Thinkers don't trust people who speak quickly. She feels the tension building and attempts to recover by engaging in small talk. He doesn't like small talk.

She continues to ramble on and he gets whiplash trying to keep up with the features and benefits she presents. He prefers someone who speaks slowly, methodically and asks questions. She hasn't researched his company, an unnecessary step she thought. She prefers to talk rather than to ask questions. The Thinker likes people who ask questions and pay attention to details. She leaves the meeting feeling good. After all she did get to talk for an hour so he must like her. He thinks I'll never work with that person. The reality is rapport is not established and this results in no sale.

In these examples, the people involved failed to understand and adjust to a personality different than theirs. In both cases, they were exact opposites. Each of these personalities process information differently and have different priorities. Your ability to adjust how you communicate with others is the most important skill of all. First, you identify and then you adjust.

Here are some adjustments to make with each personality. Keep in mind that most people in this world are not like you. They have different hot buttons, or dominant motivators than you. What is important to you is not always important to them. Other people process information differently than you. Remember, you can't change that and will be eternally frustrated when you try to. This is the way that it is!

MAGIC BULLETS

- Personality processes information in a different manner.

- You can't change a personality so it's best to learn how to adjust to it.

- You build rapport and manage tension when you adjust.

- There is always tension when people meet. Understanding personality styles helps you manage tension.

- Common ground builds rapport. Always seek to find common ground.

CHAPTER 18

Applying the Platinum Rule!

Years ago in a video program, I challenged the premise of the 'golden rule.' The Golden Rule says, "Do unto others as you would have them do unto you." Although I believe in the spirit of the golden rule for the most part it doesn't make sense to me.

If for example, I was to apply the golden rule to communicating, I'm saying communicate to others as you would have them communicate to you. Those who communicate to others the way they want to be communicated to have a narrow, ineffective perspective. They assume everyone wants to be communicated to in the same manner as they do. Those who sell to others the way they want to be sold will sell less. Unless they are selling to someone who has the same personality style as them the odds will work against them. Those who manage others the way they want to be managed have too narrow a view as well. The golden rule does not apply as the simple truth is everyone does not want to be communicated to in the same manner.

I believe in the Platinum rule. With the Platinum Rule you communicate to others the way they want to be communicated to. This same rule suggests that you sell to others as they want to be sold. When you communicate to others the way they want to be communicated to you establish rapport and achieve greater results. So how do others want you to communicate?

The Socializer likes small talk and appreciates a sense of humor. This personality is in no hurry. The feeling of trust and rapport are most important to the Socializer. They appreciate a smile and a warm friendly handshake. The Socializer likes to laugh and when they find something or someone in common there is much to talk about. It is best to let Socializers talk. This personality likes the big picture and is easily bored with details. Details are not that important to the Socializer. The Socializer tends to speak more quickly and loves people to listen. Speaking quickly is not a turn off but speaking slowly is. Socializers love to be recognized and love to be complimented in public or private. Take your time, relax and have fun and you'll both be better for it.

The Director dislikes small talk and wants you to get to the point. They appreciate strong eye contact and a firm handshake. They may crunch your hand to take control. The Director is very conscious of time. Let the Director know that you value time as well. Focus on goals, objectives and results and this personality will relate to you. Results are important to the Director. The Director will listen intently when you speak slowly and with purpose. Directors don't appreciate fast talkers. Be on time and be precise. Be conscious of time and make sure the Director understands that you are. Be direct, get to the point, focus on results and you'll be on the same wavelength.

The Thinker dislikes small talk as well. Thinkers will generally give you a weaker handshake and are less aggressive than the Director.

The Thinker appreciates punctuality and attention to detail. Focus on planning, a step-by-step plan to avoid mistakes appeals to the Thinker. Thinkers don't like mistakes. The Thinker feels manipulation more than any other personality so speak slowly and methodically. The Thinker likes it when you slow down as it gives him time to think. Thinkers are information driven and sticklers for details. Be on time, be precise, stay on track and focus on the step by step process and you'll be on the same wavelength.

The Relater loves small talk and the opportunity to relate with others. This is a soft, sensitive personality who values the relationship more than anything else. Relaters don't like loud or aggressive people and prefer a softer tone. Relaters make decisions based on the needs of others more than their own. You want to let them know you understand the importance of others. This personality feels pressure easily so slow down and soften your tone. Relaters appreciate warm eye contact and listening skills. Build rapport, soften your tone and turn on your listening skills.

A positive attitude and well developed people skills is a powerful combination. When your attitude is right you are open to learning. When you are open to learning it is easier to internalize skills that are important. When you internalize attitudinal and people skills everything is impacted in a positive way.

Your personality is unique with inherent strengths and weaknesses. Not all the strengths and weaknesses will apply to you. Some will and some won't. What is important here is to focus on the strengths you have and eliminate the weaknesses. The following is a checklist for each personality and suggestions for change. Take a pencil and check off the action steps that apply to you. In this way you will tailor your action plans for change.

The Socializer

Description: An extrovert who enjoys meeting people. The Socializer is at ease with others and loves to engage in small talk. An agile wit and a great sense of humor the Socializer loves being the centre of attention. A warm smile and a friendly manner make the Socializer popular with others. The Socializer communicates with ease and is much better at speaking than listening.

Dominant Motivator: Recognition is the dominant motivator of this personality. Socializers like to be noticed. They wear brighter colors and are conscious of how they look. The Socializer likes to drive vehicles that have 'sex appeal' focusing more on form than function. A red sports car could be perfect. Usually has strong posture.

Potential Weaknesses: Lack of planning, lack of attention to detail, makes decisions with little thought, talks too much, listens too little. Weak on follow up and follow through and has difficulty maintaining focus. Makes unrealistic time estimates and is often late as a result.

Action Plan for Change:

Write specific goals   _____

Think decisions through   _____

Plan to arrive 15 minutes early for appointments   _____

Take courses on improving your listening skills   _____

Slow down with Thinkers and Directors   _____

Take notes write it down, write it down, and write it down   _____

The Director

Description: A driver focused on achieving results. Directors dislike small talk and want to get to the point. The Director is time conscious and fears wasting time. Intense and competitive the Director likes to be in control. Likes function more than form and focuses on results. Likes to wear dark clothes and drive dark vehicles.

Dominant Motivator: Achieving goals and objectives. Likes to wear dark colors and is not above intimidating to achieve results. The Director likes to drive large, dark vehicles that symbolize power. Power is important to the Director.

Potential Weaknesses: Often perceived as an insensitive bully. Directors are considered to be overly opinionated and unaware of the feelings of others. Directors fail to appreciate the importance of recognition and emotional support.

Action Plan:

Focus more on the needs of others   _____

Stop being captain of the world and delegate   _____

Read books not related to business   _____

Soften it up with relaters   _____

Learn to recognize others, focus on your people skills   _____

Lighten up and have some fun. Smell the flowers. Don't count them!   _____

The Thinker

Description: An introvert who feels more comfortable with procedures than people. Pays close attention to detail and thinks in a step-by-step manner. The thinker is reliable, punctual and can be counted on to follow through. The thinker plans ahead to avoid surprises and usually does. This personality likes to drive energy efficient vehicles with good resale potential. Thinkers are always thinking ahead.

Dominant Motivator: The Thinker is motivated by planning and attention to detail. Dislikes wearing bright colors and prefers earth tones. The Thinker tends to be a minimalist in nature.

Potential Weaknesses: The Thinker has difficulty relating to people. They are often considered unfriendly but that is not the case. Thinkers have restricted comfort zones and have difficulty changing habits as they are prone to routine. Thinkers can get bogged down in detail and not see the bigger picture. Thinkers have tendency towards perfectionism and this leads to unrealistic expectations.

Action Plan:

Drive a different way to work, eat at a different place ____

Focus on stretching your comfort Zone (question #4) ____

Focus on your people skills, get involved with others and have fun ____

Think it through but remember to take action (question #1) ____

Pick up the pace with Socializers ____

Take a course in Public Speaking ____

Relaters

Description: An extrovert who loves people and values relationships. The Relater is a soft, sensitive person who puts the needs of others before her own. This personality tunes in easily to the feelings of others and can be an empathetic sponge. The Relater dislikes loud, aggressive people and prefers harmony in life.

Dominant Motivator: Motivated by team play and a sense of belonging. Has a high need for emotional support. Makes decisions based on how it will affect others. The Relater avoids conflict and strives for harmony. Likes to wear warm colors.

Potential Weaknesses: Relaters have difficulty making decisions as they try to please everyone. In addition, this personality lacks assertiveness. Relaters have difficulty saying no. The emotive nature of the personality can cause mood swings. The expressive nature makes the relater ramble and not get to the point. Relaters have difficulty accepting criticism.

Action Plan:

Take courses on assertiveness, learn to say no   _____

Get to the point, especially with Directors   _____

Focus on not taking things so personally   _____

Set written goals (SMART)   _____

Learn to put yourself first sometimes   _____

Work on your time management   _____

MAGIC BULLETS

- Always be aware of the personality style in direct opposition to yours.

- Socializers need more structure. Structure brings freedom.

- Directors need to have more fun. Directors can be one dimensional.

- Relaters need not be so sensitive. Learn to not take things so personally.

- Thinkers need not over analyze. Stretch your comfort zone.

CONCLUSION

Thanks for hanging in there with me. Did you read your card today? Your attitude will have the most impact on your business and your life. The objective of this writing is to help you take action. You are 21 days away from implementation. Like throwing a stone into a pond your positive attitude will have a rippling effect.

Implementation is your first important step but it is only the beginning. Your ultimate goal is internalization, making it a part of you. As we discussed change is an inside job. Once these attitudes are internalized, like riding a bike you will have them for life, a better life. You want to be focused, persistent and stick with it. There are negative forces out there trying to pull you back. You're better than that or you wouldn't have read this far. Your positive, well adjusted attitude will open many doors. It will open the doors of learning and applying as well. You'll feel the synergy and be open to new ideas and skills.

I wrote of the importance of people skills. All the other skills are meaningless without people skills. In this world you are always interacting with people. Different personalities react and process information differently. It's up to you to adjust. This skill will impact all that you do and help you communicate more effectively. Focus on the natural strengths of your personality and take action to improve on your weaknesses. You can do the most amazing things when you focus on your attitude and people skills.

Perhaps we'll meet some time as I travel across the country. I hope we do. I'd love to hear from you. My web site is **www.allanbaylis.com.** There is a four digit code on your card. With your number you will receive discounts on other products. In the event you lose a card or need anything please feel free to contact me. In the interim, I hope this book is a spark. It is you who is the flame. You are the best motivator you'll ever meet. You are *The Magic Bullet!*